The Last Stamp

The Last Stamp

by Jan Mitchell

Remembering Jimmy Mitchell

A remarkable young man

2nd edition self published by Jan Mitchell
November 2002
Printed and bound by KNI, Inc.
Manufacturer of Books
Anaheim, CA

1st edition published by StoryArts, Inc.
August 2002
123-C West Glaucus St., Leucadia, CA 92024
(760) 436.3970
e-mail: sunrich@abac.com

For copies contact Jan Mitchell at:
4102 E. Calle Redonda #46, Phoenix, AZ 85018
or e-mail Janmitchell@mycidco.com

A portion of the proceeds of this book will go to:
San Dieguito High School War Memorial Fund
San Dieguito Heritage Museum
StoryArts, Inc. Peoples Publishing and Productions

For my beloved daughter Erin,
so you never forget the love your father had for you

and

In memory of Jimmy Mitchell.

My love forever,
Mudder

February 28, 2002

Dear Erin,

When I was seventeen, I went to a movie with your dad at the old La Paloma Theater in Encinitas. The year was 1961, and the movie was "Splendor in the Grass." I had gone to see movies with him many times, but this time was different for me. When it ended we went to The Wayside Drive-In for an ice cream cone. My mind just couldn't release a scene that had taken place in a classroom with a girl about my age. Her words wouldn't leave me, and I didn't want them to leave me. And I didn't know why. I discussed it briefly with your dad. I have no idea this many years later what his response was.

I do remember many other things your dad said and did. And I do know that I have wanted to tell you about him, what a wonderful man he was and how he longed to see you. Even though I spoke to you about him through the years I always had a longing to one day write something for you — something that not only you, but your children could hold in their hands. Something that could bring him to life. My wish for you is that this book could do just that.

And oh, yes Erin, after we finished our ice cream that evening and your dad brought me home I crawled into bed that night with pen and paper in hand. It was that movie again. I needed to write down the words the young actress had recited. To this day, it is the only thing I have ever memorized and stored away without ever forgetting.

"What though the radiance which was once so bright
Be now forever taken from my sight,
Though nothing can bring back the hour
Of splendor in the grass, of glory in the flower;
We grieve not, rather find
Strength in what remains behind," ...
—Ode 'Intimations of Immortality' by William Wordsworth

All my love forever,

Your Grudder

—Table of Contents—

February, 1959
Encinitas, California

Shrieks of joy echoed off the walls in the girls' locker room at San Dieguito High School. Before anyone could inquire about my delight, I blurted out … Jimmy Mitchell followed me up the stairs in the courtyard on my way to English class last period. "He asked me to the Valentine's Dance," I said in disbelief. Sitting at our kitchen table in Hawaii, five years later, the subject of our first date came up as we ate dinner and watched Lloyd Thaxton's Teen Dance show. "You answered before I ever finished asking you out," he said laughing. I starred at him with a sheepish grin and uttered "uh huh." He was probably right.

Anyway, on the thirteenth of February, I ran around the house like a delirious fifteen-and-a-half-year-old preparing for the double date. I was dressed in a bright red dress with matching red shoes—a real Valentine! The only thing missing was one of Cupid's arrows through my rib cage. My parents must have watched in amusement. All they had heard was their only child chattering away about some star athlete named Jimmy Mitchell.

The sound of exhaust pipes on his '54 Chevy convertible backfired as it descended down the small hill to our house. This became a most familiar sound, especially to our dog, Major. There was a knock on the door, which brought a frenzy of ferocious barking from the German shepherd. As my father got up from his chair, he gave Major a command to lie down. The dog obeyed but continued to whine. My dad walked over to the door, opened it up and there stood a 5'4" stocky, blue-eyed blonde.

He had a smile from ear to ear. "Hello Mr. Bertoncini," he said while extending his hand. "I'm Jimmy Mitchell." "Come in Jimmy," my dad replied and then he introduced him to my mother. That was my clue for the grand entrance … all patiently planned ahead of time. A girl was never to look as though she were ready and waiting for her date. I had been ready and waiting at least an hour before he arrived. "Hi Jan," he said still grinning. "Hi," I responded shyly. Both my parents were good conversationalists which helped ease what I always considered the torment of the evening. My parents said later they were impressed the minute he walked through the front door. He radiated a warmhearted affection—a young man with an energetic soul.

I reached for my wrap in hopes of speeding up the introductory process. "I'll have your daughter home right after the dance, Mr. Bertoncini." He glanced at Major. The dog had quivering lips and his teeth shined like a dinosaur from another age. "Yes sir, I'll have your daughter back right after the dance," he laughed.

The gym was packed. The sound of '50s music filled the air. It didn't take us any time to catch on to each other's dance moves—it was like we had danced many lives before. It all came natural and dancing became one of our favorite pastimes.

As promised, he drove me home—straight from the dance. He walked me to the door. I eagerly waited for what I wanted most of all, a kiss from Jimmy Mitchell. Instead, he thanked me for the date and shook my hand.

The following week I had my second date, and the third, and still no kiss. Every morning at school my girlfriends were waiting for a report. "Did he kiss you yet?" "No," I responded with a shrug.

Like most of our dates, the fifth date was a basketball game. The Junior Varsity played first, and I always stayed to watch Jimmy's varsity games. As usual, the crowd was captivated with his performance. He always played the best possible game he could play. He played so intense and with such enthusiasm it would stagger the mind. I beamed with pride knowing I was his date when the game had ended.

And as always, he was extremely thirsty after each game. He would down, what seemed to me, gallons of water. He once said, "My mom has never forgotten to leave a soda on the night stand by my bed. It's always waiting for me when I come home."

After the game, he said, "Let's drive to 'Rancho.' I'm gonna take you to Blueberry Hill." Rancho Santa Fe was and still is a charming small community east of Encinitas. "Where's Blueberry Hill?" I asked. "You'll see," he replied, while finishing a can of soda.

We drove the short distance to "Rancho" winding through endless groves of eucalyptus trees. When we reached the spot, he turned off his engine. "This is it," he chuckled. "Blueberry Hill." He got out of the car and walked over to the edge of a cliff. "Jan," he called out, "come over here." I opened my door and went to the cliff. "Look at the moon," he said. While I peered through the trees, he took my hand and pulled me close to him. At last, my kiss. The romance was on!

— Acknowledgements —

I'm extremely grateful to the people who assisted me, even in some small way, in writing this book. First and foremost, a very special thank you to Tom Rodhouse for your unconditional love when I could barely pick up the pen to write. Thank you, Tommy, for your support, encouragement and editing whenever I asked for help.

And to Norm Kegerreis, I will be forever appreciative for your persistence in locating Erin and me after thinking of us for so many years.

To my "girlfriends" who were in Hawaii when I received the tragic news: JoAnn Zarfoss, Caryll Fagan, Mary Howard, Diane Petersen and Jill Myatt. Thank you for helping me recall various events of that evening and also for staying in close contact even today. Jill, you are one special lady. You never wavered in your encouragement. You persisted in convincing me not to give up "my project."

To the following people who gave of their time to answer any of my questions: Thank you, Colonel Edward Keyes Jr., USMC (Ret.); Sergeant Major Arthur "Sam" Fernandez, USMC (Ret.); Ed Paulus; Ed Beesley; Kay and Michael Vickers; Catherine "Kitty" Church; Nancy Bossidy; Jean Wilson; Mike Repp; Tim Minor; Mike Shores; David Gonzales; Colonel Brian J. Fagan, USMC (Ret.); Ed Howard, and Lieutenant General R.B. Johnston, USMC (Ret.).

To Bob Thomas and Sheila Lewis Tholl for their untiring patience in teaching me the difference between a computer mouse and a rodent. To Debbie Kendrick, you are the perfect example of loyalty. Thank you for always being available to type my manuscript over and over. You went way beyond the call of duty to help create this book, and always kept a smile. To Wendy Haskett for sharing her valuable knowledge of writing and for her perpetual optimism.

To Linda Benson and Sally Clevenger who have always supported me. To Nancy Allf who believed and stood by me. To the great team of people at StoryArts, Inc. who worked so hard for me, especially Lois Sunrich and Doris Doi.

To my mother and father who gathered information and answered questions day after day. To my son Brandon, his wife Karen, and son Jeff, who gave me their love and patience during the times that were most difficult for me. But most of all, thank you God for working through me.

— Prologue —

James McNally Mitchell Jr. was born August 8, 1940, in Seattle. He moved to Encinitas, California, with his mother and stepfather in the early 1950s. He went to San Dieguito High School starting in his sophomore year. He had a passion for sports. He was athletic and a good sport—win or lose. In no time, he made it apparent to everyone who knew him that he was a young man of confidence, integrity and selflessness. He was always optimistic. At 5'4", he was a standout on both the basketball court and football field. He had already developed into a leader.

I met Jimmy when he was a senior and I a sophomore. If there is such a thing as love at first sight, then that is what happened to me on that February day in 1959. Our courtship lasted throughout high school and his college years. He always said he had a dream of being a Marine or a coach. He enrolled in the Marine Corps Platoon Leader's Class while attending Palomar College. He graduated from San Diego State in 1963. He spent most of two summers in Quantico, Va., attending the PLC program. He was commissioned a Second Lieutenant the day he graduated from San Diego State. We were engaged Christmas Eve 1963. April 18, 1964, we were married in a military wedding in Del Mar, California.

His first duty station was to be at the Marine Corps Air Station, Kaneohe, Hawaii. It was all like a dream come true. When we arrived that May, we found the idyllic house one block from the beach at 430 North Kalaheo in Kailua, a few miles from the Air Station. The house sat on a cement slab painted ping pong green. It had two small bedrooms and a large yard with plumerias and our very own coconut tree. Rent was $150 per month. Jimmy's salary was $222 a month plus allowances. But we thought we had it all. Surfing, long walks collecting sea shells and green glass balls that had drifted to shore from the fishermen's nets, and wonderful friends to share in the fun.

When I announced he was going to be a father, he was thrilled. The baby was due August 1. At that point, we knew nothing of the events which were to take him away. The planning and preparation for a two-week exercise on the

California coast turned into what would become a one-year-plus separation for all Marines and their families. Instead, they were sent to Okinawa in preparation for their beach landing at Chu Lai, South Vietnam. I heard his voice for the last time by short wave radio from Okinawa. I heard him say for the last time, "I love you." They arrived at Chu Lai on May 7, 1965.

Jimmy's greatest dream was to hold his baby girl. He was killed by shrapnel wounds 42 days after Erin was born.

Jimmy Mitchell
Chu Lai, Vietnam, 1965

May 1965
Janny …

    A man from my platoon was over talking to a friend of his from the 1st Platoon and somehow the fellow from the first platoon accidentally discharged a bullet into a man from my platoon. The corpsman did everything he could but he died before we could get him to the hospital. It was an accident but what a price to pay for a stupid mistake. It happened just before dark, about 7:00. It is the first time I have ever seen anyone die and it makes one really stop and wonder what this is all about.

Jimmy Mitchell
Chu Lai, South Vietnam, 1965

*It is not what he has, nor even what he does,
which directly expresses the worth of a man,
but what he is.*

—Henri Frederic Amiel

COMPANY "D"
1st Battalion, 4th Marines (-)(Rein)
3rd Marine Division (Rein), FMF
c/o FPO, San Francisco 96601

1 September 1965

Mrs. Janet B. Mitchell
c/o Mrs. William C. G. Church
665 Ulumalu Street
Kailua, Oahu, Hawaii

My dear Mrs. Mitchell:

It is with deepest regret that I write you about the untimely death of your husband, First Lieutenant James M. Mitchell, U. S. Marine Corps, on 31 August 1965 near Chu Lai, Republic of Vietnam. His death is a source of great sorrow to me, the officers and the men of this company and his many friends in the 1st Battalion, 4th Marines. Please accept our heartfelt sympathy in your bereavement.

Jim was on a daylight combat patrol near the Chu Lai airfield, when the lead element of his platoon found an anti-personnel mine. He went forward to investigate the report. When Jim arrived at the scene an undiscovered mine exploded. He received multiple wounds and was rendered unconscious. Immediately Jim received attention from the Navy Medical Corpsman present and was removed to a field aid station via helicopter. Despite all the efforts of the medical officers at the aid station, Jim never regained consciousness and died at 11:00 o'clock A.M. on 31 August 1965. Father Dowd, a Navy Chaplain who was at the aid station, administered the sacrament of Extreme Unction to him. I am sure it will be of some comfort to you to know that a Requiem Mass will be said for Jim in the company area on 2 September 1965.

Jim's integrity and devotion to duty won for him the respect of all who knew him. As Jim's company commander, I considered him my most competent and reliable platoon commander. I believe the reason he was so successful as a platoon commander was because of the mutual respect that existed between him and his men. Being an infantry platoon commander is not a job, or even a profession; it is a way of life. Jim lived that way of life in a manner which was exemplary to all of us. As his wife I know that you shared the hardship of separation. However, I hope you will remember only the pleasant periods as we do. You and Erin were always in his thoughts and constantly the subject of our conversations. Although I realize that words can do little to console you in your grief, I earnestly hope the knowledge that Jim is keenly missed by his many friends will in some measure alleviate your sadness.

If I can be of any assistance to you, please do not hesitate to write me.

Sincerely,

ROBERT M. SWEENEY
Captain, U. S. Marine Corps
Commanding

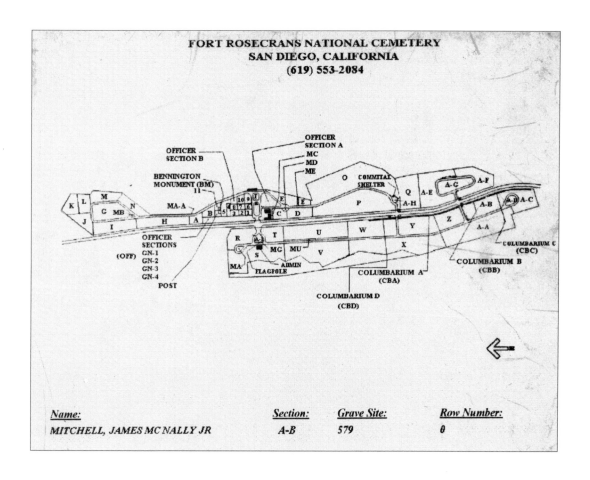

FORT ROSECRANS NATIONAL CEMETERY
SAN DIEGO, CALIFORNIA
(619) 553-2084

Name:	Section:	Grave Site:	Row Number:
MITCHELL, JAMES MC NALLY JR	A-B	579	0

14

— His Burial —

September 1965

His mother sat in the middle, his stepfather to the left of her. I sat to the right and gave her hand a squeeze as the hearse led the procession out of Del Mar. We made the long climb up the scenic hill overlooking the ocean through Torrey Pines on old Highway 101.

This is his last ride on 101. We drove here on our first date. I always snuggled close to him in his '54 light blue Chevy convertible. I asked him how much longer it would be before we could get married. I asked him that question right here where we're driving. He said, "I need more money in my savings account." He laughed; I pouted.

The procession continued. We curved around what seemed like endless hills, and we were there. We were there because I saw hundreds and hundreds of white grave markers. We were at Fort Rosecrans National Cemetery, seated on the bluff of Point Loma, California, overlooking the Pacific Ocean. I remember it was a sunny Southern California day. The sun had broken through the morning fog. The sound of an airplane in the far distance added to my feelings of loss. There were people and cars everywhere.

The family priest gave the eulogy. I don't remember what he said. My mind was riveted on a huge wreath in front of us. It seemed to represent everything at that moment. It was a wreath of red gladiolas dressed with white China mums and ti leaves. In the center was inscribed "SON." After the eulogy, the honor guard of Marines fired a rifle volley. Taps were played. They removed the flag from the casket, folded it, and presented it to me. The ceremony was over. I stood and waited for most everyone to leave, and then I walked over to the silver box. I kissed the tips of my fingers and pressed them to the coffin. "Goodbye," I whispered. "I'll see you again some day." I turned toward the black car. Now for the first time, my grief was replaced with anger.

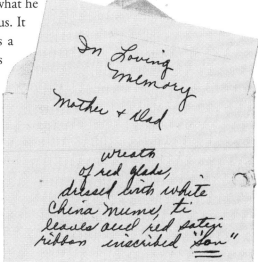

— Our Relationship —

Jimmy and I began dating in February 1959 ...

"Jan, would you like to go to the Valentine's Dance with me? We could go to Pernicano's afterward for a pizza. Bill's asking Ingrid, and we'll double date."

February

13 Coronado at S. D., Basketball
    Girls' League Assembly
6   Vista at S. D., Basketball
10 S. D. at Fallbrook, Basketball
    Pictures for clubs - for annual
11 National Assembly
13 Intermediate Tri-Hi-Y Dance
    Art Club Cake Sale
17 Mar Vista at S. D., Basketball

San Dieguito High School,

Encinitas, California

LASAGNA

SPAGHETTI   ANTIPASTO SALAD   RAVIOLI

PERNICANO'S
FAMOUS ORIGINAL
PIZZA HOUSE
of La Jolla

711 Turquoise   HU 8-2900

Take Out Orders

BEER   7 LOCATIONS   WINE

1st date

JIM MITCHELL
Track 1, 2
V. Football 2, 3, 4
V. Basketball 2, 3, 4
A. S. B. Act Mgr. 4
Class Pres. 4
Lettermen's Club
Hi-Y Club
Prom Comm. 3
Senior Class Representative 4

Jimmy Mitchell
Senior Picture, 1959

J. V. Cheerleaders

Jan Bertoncini (MITCHELL)
your wife

Mitchell tries for more as opposing tackler closes in.

Senior Officers

Second Semester Officers: Row 1: J. Mitchell, Rep.; B. Nelson, Treas. Row 2: J. Price, Pub. Mgr.; A. Wright, President; G. Amtmann, Act. Mgr. Not pictured: A. Lyman, Vice Pres.; V. Gann, Sec.

Senior Athlete Honor Goes to Jim Mitchell

Jim Mitchell was presented the Senior Athlete of the Year award last Wednesday night at the annual San Dieguito High sports banquet in the high school cafeteria.

One of the most successful sports years in San Dieguito's history was climaxed by this well-attended banquet, open to any boy who had participated in any of the school sports the past season, their fathers and members of the pep squad.

The Senior Athlete of the Year award was a fitting ending to Mitchell's brilliant three year varsity career at San Dieguito. Mitchell, the "Mighty Mite," made up for the lack of size —5.4. — 140 pounds — with tremendous coordination, quickness afoot and an unquenchable desire to win. He never stopped hustling.

Mitchell opened his senior year on the gridiron. There, as a speedy halfback he helped spark the Mustangs to a co-championship and a post-season playoff game. Mitchell led the team in total offense with 623 yards, 447 rushing and 176 on pass receptions. He was also second in scoring with 56. Proof of his sparkling play was given when he was named to the all-league first eleven.

From the gridiron, Mitchell moved to the hardwoods for another great season. He was named to the all-tournament five in the Kiwanis tournament, was "best defensive player" at the Banning tourney, and was the team's second highest scorer with 172 points. Again he was named to the all-league team. His biggest award for basket-ball, however, came when coach Paul Pruett named him Most Valuable Player.

Mitchell added to his laurels by lettering in track, where he ran the sprints and broad jumped.

Ernie Hylton, who announces all of San Dieguito's home football games, presented the trophy to Mitchell. A huge permanent trophy remains in the school trophy case.

Jim Mitchell

'Mitch' Shines in Varsity Games

Out of the small world of sports here at San Dieguito, we hear and see so much nowadays of one who is rapidly growing in skill and popularity. We are speaking of Jim Mitchell who is a short but fast guard playing for the Mustang Varsity Basketball Team.

Jim, who is a sophomore, is 5'3" and weighs a stocky 135 pounds. He is a fast and promising guard paying his first year of High School Basketball.

Jim is well known and talked about among the Basketball enthusiasts. Also, with two years yet to go, we will be seeing and hearing a lot more about this great little colt size mustang.

Jimmy asked me to his senior prom. The night he came to pick me up was unforgettable. Unforgettable because he and our dog Major had never made peace with one another. Jimmy and I were both devoted animal lovers but I think he sensed early on that our German shepherd was very protective of our family and would never give an inch! This was confirmed when the milkman, who wasn't quite as quick and agile as Jimmy, lost the seat of his pants one early crisp morning, running back to his milk truck.

On the night of the prom we could hear Jimmy's Chevy approaching our house. My mother was at the window and thought the dog was in the bedroom. Jimmy got out of his car, walked a short distance toward the front door, and then it happened. The dog came racing around the corner of the house. In an instant Jimmy turned, ran toward his car and made a perfectly clean dive through the open passenger window. My father instantly ran outside. Jimmy was sitting in his car; windows rolled up, laughing hysterically. Eventually I did get my corsage. It was gardenias, and he escorted me to the car in his white tux—my mother following directly behind with her 8-mm movie camera!

The Class of 1960

presents the

Junior - Senior

Prom

May 23, 1959
9:00 - 1:00

La Jolla Country Club

$3.00

Going to the Colorado River on the outskirts of Blythe, California, was probably at the top of our list for fun. It was an annual event that usually lasted five or six days depending if we could last five or six days. My family's relatives and friends had been making the trip several years before I met Jimmy. Once we were dating, he was instantly included in the group. He absolutely loved these trips from beginning to end.

We'd pack my father's '57 blue Chevrolet pickup truck with cots, food, lanterns, a tent and anything else that went with camping. After all the gear was in place, the two of us would climb in the back of the truck, cover up with blankets and make the three-and-a-half-hour trip sneaking kisses all the way.

Once we'd arrive we'd all make the comment, "Man, it's hot." Temperatures usually ranged anywhere from 105 to 116 degrees. We would unpack, set up, camp and jump in the river. If we weren't skiing, we would have my dad or Uncle John take us up river to the weir. We would jump from the boat with our inner tubes and float down the river back to camp usually taking about 45 minutes.

At night we would wrap ourselves in a water soaked cold sheet not only to cool us off but also to ward off the masses of mosquitoes while we tried to get a few hours sleep on our cot. In the morning, we were awakened with a magnitude of flies. The only luxury was a restroom and small snack shop on the park grounds.

The highlight of the trip was my father pulling five skiers at one time with his Mercury 40 horsepower motor. It was no small feat. After several unsuccessful trips my dad succeeded in getting us all up at one time by starting with one or two of us at a time on the skis and then circling around and picking up one or two of us with a running start until all five were skiing.

Later, when my folks came to Hawaii on their first visit, we all sat on the living room floor huddled around our small fan reminiscing about our river days. We laughed until we had tears rolling down our cheeks.

Jimmy and I grew closer and closer. And as the months passed, I became even more aware of who he was. He never ceased to amaze me with his sincere concern for others. He was always for the underdog. He had an inner driving force which aided others in improving themselves. If a coach was giving a guy a tongue lashing, Jimmy would always take the guy aside and lend a word of encouragement. He would stay after school if necessary. He never gave up on those he could help. To me, he seemed way beyond his 18 years.

During part of the summers, Jimmy would drive to Orienda, California, to stay with his father and stepmother Betty and his half-brothers, John and Leo. There was always a job waiting for him at Todd Shipyards in Alameda on the San Francisco Bay. Besides working in Alameda his father was a college football referee. On one occasion, we drove together so I could meet the rest of his family. It was a special trip, and everyone made me feel welcome.

June 10, 1959
Jimmy's Senior Commencement and Graduation

Front, left to right: John, Jimmy, and Leo. Back: Jim, Sr. with wife Betty.

A Surprise Gift

I opened the small box and gazed at the necklace. I was young, in love, and celebrating my 17th birthday. I reached for the chain that held the small glass ball and examined it carefully. Inside the glass there appeared to be a tiny seed. Reaching over I placed my hand upon his shoulder and kissed him lightly on the cheek. He was my high school sweetheart and I adored him. I took the necklace home and proudly showed my parents. I was not aware of its significance. I only knew it was from him to me.

Jan Marie Bertoncini
September 26, 1960

Matthew 17:20
For truly I say to you / if you have faith as a mustard seed, you shall say to this mountain, / move from here to there and it shall move: and nothing shall be impossible to you.

December, 1959

"Janny, will you go with me? My dad's going to drive down from Orienda. He'll be one of the referees."
"I'll call you back."
(5 minutes or less).
"My dad says I can go, Jimmy."

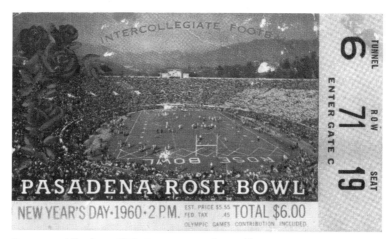

Once, around Christmas, 1959, Jimmy surprised me with a pair of tickets to the game.

In 1960, he started his two-year course at Palomar Junior College. Again, he was a standout on the basketball court. Crowds were fascinated with his incredible speed and agility. His nickname was "weasel." He got the name in high school for his sly and vigorous moves on the floor. He was known by that name to many friends, teammates and opponents. If his lack of height and size for such sports as basketball and football ever bothered him, I never knew it. No one else did either. He worked hard to prove that size was never a factor in his performance.

Sometime in the spring of 1961, Jimmy enrolled in the Platoon Leaders Course of the Marine Corps. The course was designed to develop officers. He attended the first six-week session in the summer of 1961 and the second six-week session in the summer of 1962. The schools were at Quantico, Va., and it was tough having him so far away for so long. Each time he returned, I was ecstatic.

After graduating from Palomar, he went to San Diego State.

When Jimmy left home and got an apartment in San Diego with several other students I had some insecurities about our relationship ending. We'd part on Sunday evenings, and he'd drive back to school. The following Friday I would wait (and not patiently) for his call saying he had arrived home. Some Friday nights we went our own direction. We both had other friends and never isolated ourselves from any of them. Saturday nights were "ours." After a date, we would go to the popular Wayside Drive-In, then located on Highway 101 and K Street in Encinitas. We would order the usual chocolate ice cream cone, swap stories with friends about the evening and then it was home … promptly at midnight.

Sundays we would head for Moonlight Beach. He always parked his Chevy in the same location. He would back it under a certain old cypress tree. The tree still stands today with only a few branches remaining. It's weather-worn aged appearance brings back so many memories. Friends would gather around, and he'd put the top down on his car. And if Fats Domino's "Blueberry Hill" came on the radio, you can be sure the volume went up.

In between surfing and swimming he would play volleyball with his buddies, and I would join my "regulars" to surf (or attempt it) and soak up sun. In those days there was a snack bar on the beach with music playing from outside speakers. Once in a while a song would come on that we both liked to dance to. I would raise my head from the beach towel, and we would connect with a grin during his volley ball game.

He received a degree in business administration in June 1963. Graduation day was an exciting time for all, including my parents and his. Besides graduating from college, he was commissioned a Second Lieutenant into the United States Marine Corps. President John F. Kennedy was the commencement speaker. When the ceremony ended, we watched as the president made his way into the helicopter while slightly bumping his head as he went through the door. Almost all television sets of that time were black and white. The images on those televisions gave people a gray shadowy appearance. When we saw JFK in person, the color of his hair was somewhat of a surprise. We commented how red it appeared. It wasn't the color we had imagined. It was a thrill to see the President for that one brief moment.

RESERVED

San Diego State College
Commencement

Speaker: The President of the United States

June 6, 1963

Please present this card before 11:00 a.m.
No reservations held after 11:00 a.m.

Nº 8074 **RESERVED**

June 5, 1963

"Congratulations Lieutenant Mitchell! You have worked so hard these past four years. What a privilege to pin on your 'gold bars.'"

Jan

THE
PRESIDENT
OF
THE UNITED STATES OF AMERICA

To all who shall see these presents, greeting:

Know Ye, that reposing special trust and confidence in the patriotism, valor, fidelity and abilities of ⸻ James B. Mitchell, Jr. 087375 ⸻, I do appoint him a ⸻ Second Lieutenant ⸻ in the

Reserve of the United States Marine Corps

James McNally Mitchell, Jr.

Lieutenant
United States Marine Corps

December 1963

There was a knock on the door. He was home from The Basic School for Christmas. My family had a fire burning in the living area, and the air smelled of pine from the little tree with red lights. We sat around the fire and talked about his time at Quantico, the water skiing trips to the Colorado River and our famous card game of hearts—the loser always had to grate the cheese and onion for my mother's delicious Mexican dinners. There was laughter and reminiscing, and then it was time to exchange a Christmas gift. I can't remember what I gave him. His gift to me was a very large box, and I couldn't imagine what it could be. When I opened it, I was speechless. I looked at my parents—they already knew. I turned to him, and he had a grin from ear to ear. I grabbed him, kissed him and ran to the phone to announce to my friends the silver diamond ring.

MISS JAN BERTONCINI
. . . future bride

D2 Sun., Jan. 5, 1964 **THE SAN DIEGO UNION**
SAN DIEGO, CALIFORNIA

STRAWS IN THE WIND

Miss Bertoncini, Lt. J. M. Mitchell Are Betrothed

By EILEEN JACKSON

Days of the Dons in Southern California is recalled with the announcement of the engagement of Miss Jan Marie Bertoncini, daughter of Mr. and Mrs. Ernest Bertoncini of Encinitas, and 2nd Lt. James M. Mitchell, USMC, son of Mrs. P. A. McDonald of Encinitas. His father is James Mitchell of Orinda, Calif.

The bride-elect is the great-great-great-granddaughter of Don Juan Maria Osuna, first alcalde (mayor) of the newly-formed pueblo of San Diego in 1834. He received a grant to Rancho San Dieguito (renamed Rancho Santa Fe) two years later. In the alcalde election, Don Juan Maria Osuna defeated Pio Pico, who later became governor of California.

On her maternal side the bride-elect is granddaughter of Mr. and Mrs. Arthur L. Knipe, who have lived in Encinitas 30 years.

Eileen Jackson

Miss Bertoncini also is the great-great-granddaughter of Philip Crosthwaite, born Dec. 27, 1825, in Athy, County Kildare, Ireland. Mr. Crosthwaite held a number of offices in San Diego in the early days. He was the first county treasurer, deputy sheriff for several years and sheriff, school commissioner in 1850, county clerk and recorder in 1853-54 and justice of the peace in 1854. He was the grandfather of Mrs. Ruth Bertoncini, grandmother of the bride, who was born in the original Osuna ranch house at Rancho Santa Fe. The ranch house, now owned by Mr. and Mrs. George Willoughby, formerly was owned by Bing Crosby and later the John Howes.

Miss Jan Marie Bertoncini, w
ment to Lt. James M. Mitchell i

The bride-elect, just returned from a two-month vacation in Hawaii, was graduated from San Deiguito High School and attended San Diego Medical and Dental assistants college.

Lt. Mitchell, is a graduate of San Dieguito High School, Palomar Junior College, and San Diego State. He is attending Officers Training School in Quantico, Va. from which he will be graduated in March.

Engagement Is Announced

ENCINITAS — At a family gathering on Christmas Eve, Mr. and Mrs. Ernest Bertoncini of 1045 Neptune avenue, announced the engagement of their daughter, Miss Jan Marie Bertoncini, to United States Marine Corps Lieutenant James M. Mitchell.

The future bride is a graduate of San Dieguito Union High School and of San Diego Medical and Dental College. Prior to her recent trip to Hawaii, Miss Bertoncini was employed in the offices of a Oceanside pediatrician.

Lt. Mitchell is the son of Mrs. P. A. McDonald of 1674 Crest drive, and James McNally Mitchell, Sr., of Orinda, Calif. A graduate of San Dieguito, Lt. Mitchell is also a graduate of Palomar Junior College and San Diego State College. He is presently attending the Quantico, Va., Officer's Candidate School.

No date has been set for the wedding.

Jimmy returned to The Basic School after the holidays. By February 1964, I flew back to Quantico to be with him. We took long walks in the bitter cold. I knew he would be finishing up his Officer's Training in March and would be assigned to a duty station—neither of us knew where. After much discussion, we settled on the date of April 18, 1964, for our wedding. When I arrived home to break the news, my mother almost fainted. "Jan, that is only two months away." I called Colonel and Mrs. McDonald. They were ecstatic! As usual, my mother pulled it off.

Mr. and Mrs. Ernest Andrew Bertoncini
request the honour of your presence
at the marriage of their daughter
Jan Marie
to
Lieutenant James McNally Mitchell, Jr.
United States Marine Corps
on Saturday, the eighteenth of April
Nineteen hundred and sixty-four
at twelve o'clock noon
St. James Catholic Church
Del Mar, California

Reception
immediately following the ceremony
1045 Neptune Avenue
Encinitas, California

After the wedding ceremony we took a limo to my parents' home for the large reception. My uncle rode in the car with us. I remember sitting in the back, and we were squeezing hands. We looked at each other with a smile—and said, "Well, we did it!"

After a honeymoon at Lake Tahoe, California, we were flown to our first duty station—Hawaii. We flew via Military Airlift Command (MAC). Once there, we were given temporary housing until we found a place to live. We stayed at The Capri Motel a few blocks away from Waikiki. It didn't take us long to find the house we had dreamed about. A lieutenant and his family had just moved onto base housing and word spread to Jimmy that it was available. When we saw it, we looked at one another with a smile of approval. There was nothing more to say.

430 North Kalaheo
Kailua, Hawaii

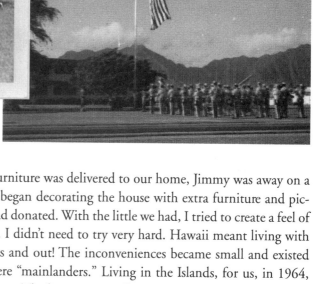

Marine Corps Air Station,
Kaneohe Bay, Hawaii

In our backyard, 1964

The day our furniture was delivered to our home, Jimmy was away on a training mission. I began decorating the house with extra furniture and pictures our parents had donated. With the little we had, I tried to create a feel of the tropics indoors. I didn't need to try very hard. Hawaii meant living with nature both indoors and out! The inconveniences became small and existed only because we were "mainlanders." Living in the Islands, for us, in 1964, was living out a dream. The house eventually came together with an Oriental rug, sofa, chair and a black and white television set with 2 or 3 "snowy" channels.

Being a wife, and a military wife, was a completely new experience. The first movie we went to was at the base theater. It was about a group who called themselves "The Beatles." The cost was 10 cents per person. I was not prepared for the event preceding the movie. The United States flag came on the screen and everyone stood at attention, hand over heart. The National Anthem was played. It was touching, and I had "goose bumps" on my arms. Suddenly, I was in a group that had pride! Just driving through the main gate getting a snappy salute from the military police made me proud to be the wife of a marine.

Jan and Jim

Our free time was spent at the beach. We had both surfed a lot when we were living in California. He had shipped his surfboard with our other things. Surfing was not great on the windward side of the Island. However, that didn't prevent either of us from sharing his board and sitting for long periods of time just to catch a decent wave. On occasion, the wind would change, and we would get choice swells.

On one of our beach walks we spotted a large glorious piece of smooth, silvery colored driftwood the sea had created. Between the two of us we brought it to shore and took it home. We put it on our front porch making the charming piece of wood a bench. We relaxed in the evenings sipping glasses of iced tea on our new bench. Our conversation was usually about the Marine Corps with an occasional "Remember when we did this or that back home?" And once he gave me a little punch in the side and said, "You're doing a good job, Janny. You're faithful in making my favorite peanut butter cookies and iced tea." I had also promised him to be faithful in getting up with him each morning and making his favorite breakfast — a fried hamburger patty and a portion of canned fruit cocktail. I never broke my promise.

— Departure —

Iremember standing outside on the small front porch of our house. Jimmy's mother, Luella, hugged him. Her lips quivered. His stepfather, Peter, shook his hand and gave him a warm slap on the back. At that moment, the neighbor who lived behind us drove by and yelled out to Jimmy, "Keep your head down bud."

Jimmy raised his fist and gave it a slight shake. He was smiling and yelled back, "I will and thanks."

Even then none of us knew for sure how long the men would be gone or exactly where they were going. One rumor had it that they would be going to the California coast for a two-week exercise. His parents exchanged a few more words of encouragement, and we were on our way to the base where we would meet with friends, Ed and Mary Howard. When we arrived, they were in the parking lot. Jimmy and I got into their car, and we talked a bit. There were tears. I was four months pregnant, and Jimmy held me close and gently patted my stomach. He reminded me, as he had many times before, to take good care of the baby. Fighting back the tears, we embraced.

Clinging to one another, we whispered our "I love yous," then parted with a moment of hesitancy. It was hard to believe he was leaving, and we had only been married for one year. I cried. They boarded the bus to Pearl Harbor. The future was now uncertain.

HEADQUARTERS
1st Marine Brigade, Fleet Marine Force
c/o FPO, San Francisco 96601

47/ges
10 March 1965

From: Commanding General
To: Colonel E. P. DUPRAS 07927/9906 USMC (RU 13151)

Subj: Movement Orders

Ref: (a) CB FMFPac msg 100210Z/Mar 1965 NOTAL

1.   Commencing on or about 11 March 1965, and in accordance with reference (a), and the embarkation schedule issued by separate instructions. the following units under your command will embark on board ships of TG 14.3 for surface transportation to WestPac for debarkation and movement to such places as may be designated:

I drove back to our little white house near the ocean, at 430 North Kalaheo. Jimmy's mother and his stepfather were waiting as the small blue Corvair entered the carport. They had arrived Saturday, six days before Jimmy departed. Peter and Jimmy had a mutual fondness for discussing Peter's career as a Marine. Peter was born in Boston in 1904 and enlisted in the Marine Corps as a private in 1922. He was commissioned a Second Lieutenant in January 1930 and was in Shanghai, China, in 1934–1935 with the 4th Marine Regiment, the same regiment Jimmy served in while in Hawaii and Vietnam. The 4th Marines were in some ways the envy of the rest of the Marine Corps because of their service in China in the 1920s and 1930s. To have been known as a "China Marine" was a source of pride. He was also a veteran of the campaign for Guam and the Palau Operation as a member of the Third Amphibions Corps in World War II. He served in most of the far-flung posts of the Marine Corps as well as the Corps' "HUB" at Washington, D.C. By the time he retired in the 1950s, he was a full Colonel. Both his parents did their utmost to maintain a cheery atmosphere in the house, but they knew the grave danger that lay ahead.

Colonel Peter McDonald
4th Marine Regiment—Shanghai China, 1934

The rest of the day we relaxed. We chatted as I heated up the leftover spaghetti from the night before. We prayed this would be over shortly, and life would be back to normal. At that point in time, no one could or would tell us how long the Hawaii Marines would be gone. There were promises: Lt. General V. H. Krulak, the Pacific Commander, told the families of the Brigade that the Brigade was being sent to Okinawa as "backup" to the Third Marine Division. Later, Secretary of Defense McNamara boasted the troops would be home by Christmas; nothing was definite.

Jimmy's mother and I went shopping the following day to look for maternity clothes. I barely hit the scales at 100 pounds, but was beaming with pride over the fact I was expecting. I wanted the world to notice I was going to be a mother; the maternity clothes would confirm it.

The remainder of their stay we exchanged stories, shopped at the commissary and toured the island. After their visit, I drove them to the airport.

To Okinawa At Sea 1965
24 March 1965
Dear Janny:

Well, it's been a long trip and uneventful with the exception of our second day out of port. I woke in the morning and found that I could not stay out of bed for more than about two minutes. The reason being, I had an upset stomach. Or as your dad would say, "Are you going to put your stomach?" or as Mike and Ed would say, "You're seasick." It lasted all day, and the following day I began to feel myself.

That Sunday we left was a long day. We finally got aboard ship about 11 that night. We sailed out of Pearl Harbor the following morning about 7:00. We are due to arrive in Okinawa tomorrow morning and will start unloading the ship, which will take about three days. There is still no word as to whether this is a temporary or permanent change.

How is Erick Peter or Cindy Lu? I bet you have gotten a little rounder in the past 10 days. When did my folks leave? I hope they were a help to you and also company for you. If this should turn out to be a temporary stay and we are not back until after the baby is born, I hope your family can come to help you.

Well, I'm in the rack now after a great dinner and a movie. Not too long and I will be looking at Okinawa tomorrow morning. I love you Janny and hope you are taking good care of yourself.

Love, Jimmy

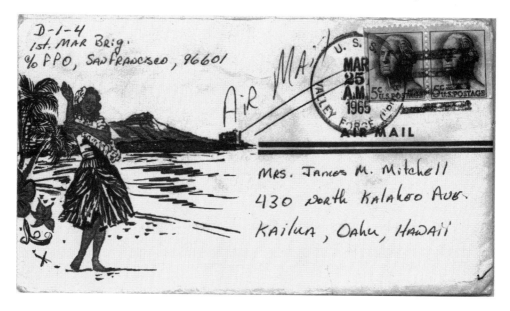

When I returned home this time, the house had an emptiness I felt in every room.

As the days passed, my girlfriends and I exchanged any new information we received which was pertinent to our husbands' return. Throughout his tour of duty, none of Jimmy's letters *ever* discussed the details of the war. He focused only on getting home and seeing his family. Every day I waited in anticipation to see the mailman walk into the side carport and knock on the kitchen door.

Knowing that I must keep busy, I started concentrating on how I would decorate the baby's room. I felt certain we would have a boy. We had even decided on the name of Erik Peter. I took a sewing class and made blue curtains. An old chest of drawers in the laundry room was painted white. I bought an area rug to cover the green cement floor and a white crib that I filled with small stuffed animals.

At night I would stay at Mary's house. My girlfriend Jill and her six-month-old baby girl, Jamy, were also staying there. In spite of the circumstances, there was always humor in the evenings. We would huddle around the television set once a week to watch the popular series "Peyton Place." We played with little Jamy, and I could hardly wait for my own baby's arrival. Our other friends would sometimes join us at night, and the house came alive with laughter. We were a close-knit group.

Okinawa, 3 April 1965
Dear Jan:

Just a short note to fill you in on the "haps." There is still no word on when or if we will be getting back to Hawaii in the near future. You had better plan on staying right where you are. I love you hon—and as you know, miss you. Take good care of yourself and (?).

Love, Jimmy

23 April 1965

… I wish I could tell you what's happening, but at this stage of the game I'm not too sure myself. All I can say is read the papers daily, and maybe one of those patrols going out will be my platoon …

Love and Kisses, Jimmy

14 April 1965
Dear Janny:

In four days we will have been married one year. I only wish that we could be together to enjoy the occasion.

I want to wish you a Holy Easter and a Happy Anniversary. I hope you received the gift I sent and that you enjoyed them.

By the way, if I haven't already mentioned it, Jim Peterson is my roomy. Ed Howard is just next door. Am still enjoying the cookies.

Love you honey, Jimmy

Easter Sunday, 18 April 1965
Dear Wife:

Just think—one year ago today we said "I do" and I am sure happy we did it then. I only wish we could be together to do it up right. I just returned from church and went to communion and thought of you and the baby praying that you both are well ...

To Vietnam, 1 May 1965
Dear "Bert":

... Well, it won't be long now. Have been at sea for about three days and expecting to land soon. Things don't look too good as far as the Viet Cong are concerned but then you can't expect them to throw up their hands and give us the place ...

I am sorry I didn't get to write before leaving Okinawa, but a couple of days before leaving, I was called to help load one of the ships and as a result, did not have much time to do anything. I love you very much Jan and hope it won't be too long until we can be back together again in our little casa on N. Kalaheo. As far as a name for the baby, if it is a girl, name her whatever you wish ...

Love you Jan, Jimmy

12 May 1965
Dear Janny Bird …

Well, we finally made it, and this is the nearest place to Hell I have seen since we left the Colorado River. My platoon is located about 1 miles down the road from the Battalion Command Post on a small sand dune. The sun comes out, and the temp must rise to about 105. There is no shade on the hill, so we have to erect shelters with our ponchos. All day long we sit in the best shade we can find and roast to death. At night we keep half the platoon awake to prevent any V.C. from coming through our lines …

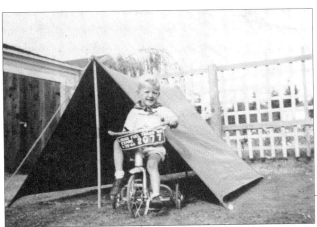

Jimmy,
Seattle, Washington
1945

Jimmy,
Chu Lai, Vietnam
1965

5 July 1965
Dear Janny,

Received your letter with the pictures enclosed last night after dark so had to wait until this morning to read it. Enjoyed the letter as usual and the pictures. The chest looks real cute and you do also fatty. The baby's room also looks great.

We are still pushing quite hard every day with little rest. Our sweep operation the other day did not go off as well as I would have liked it to. I had two men injured by a booby trap. A mine or grenade blew up throwing shrapnel into the leg of one man and into the arms, chest and leg of the other. They were quite lucky in that the injury was not real serious. They were both able to walk out to be helio evacuated. I went down to see them this morning and they are all smiles, should be back in the company in 2 weeks?

I hope this war comes to an end soon but it doesn't look as though it will …

8 July 1965, 12 noon
Dear Janny,

It's another hot one today. I tried to lie down and get a couple of hours sleep but it's just too hot.

While I am thinking of it, in your next little goody-box would you please send about 3 sets of silver bars, the small ones that go on the collar? Also put a couple of ball-point pens in the box please. Please send some notebook filler also. I will enclose a sample. These are the only little things I need at the present time.

There is not too much new around here. We have been going on about two sweeps a week. This is where a couple of companies will be put into an area by helicopter and then move through the area pushing as many V.C. as possible into another unit which is used as a blocking force. It is usually very hot and tiring.

I still have no word as to when we will be going back to Oki. There are plenty of rumors of course but I won't believe them until I am boarding the ship or plane.

I am getting rather tired of this type of life and will be happy when we leave this place. We had mass today at our Company area and I received communion and prayed for you and the baby.

I sure do miss you Jan and didn't realize how lonely it would be without you. I look for mail from you every day and am so happy when a letter arrives.

It seems as though we have been apart a year already. We are scheduled for a larger operation coming up this Saturday and Sunday. They will be two long hot days. I am really getting tired of all this stuff. Not much rest to be had and all your energy is taken from you during the hot sunny day.

I expected a letter from you today, am still hoping that as usual the mail doesn't come out until dark. This of course means I won't get to read it until morning. But it doesn't stop me from dreaming.

I love you so much honey and I am also getting anxious to be a dad. Hope all goes well. Write real often and let me know how you are feeling.

Love, James

15 July 1965, 5 o'clock
Dear Janny,

Well I'm just about fed-up to my ears with this place. They tell you you're going to do something and an hour later the word changes. The troops are being pushed to their limit as far as lack of sleep is concerned. Every now and then I have a man go to sleep on his feet at night when on patrol.

We have been going day and night with very little sleep. Maybe 4 to 5 hours. Some men don't get that. We have started platoon size patrols again instead of squads. They are run at night. We have defensive positions dug in around the strip and patrol out to their front at night.

Still don't know when we are leaving this hell box. Tomorrow wouldn't be too soon. Things are really different in my way of thinking as far as enjoying life. We are really going to live.

Please be real careful honey when you go out on the roads and don't over do it. You will have to take it real easy after you have the baby. Don't over do anything and get plenty of rest. I sure miss you honey and think of you day and night. Your folks should be there soon.

Must go to chow now—will write later if I have a chance. We have a patrol tonight leaving at 6:30 p.m. going out to an area for the night and returning about 6 in the morning. No slack Jack!!

I bet you are really getting excited now. I sure am. Please be careful honey …

I love you, Jim

At some point in April, a meeting was called on base. My friends and I attended. We were informed our husbands were going to Vietnam. Shortly thereafter, I began to make plans to return to California.

Erin's arrival

My parents arrived in Hawaii in mid-July to help me prepare for the move and to be there for the birth of the baby. My due date was August 1st. I surprised everyone by going to Tripler Army Hospital at 10:00 p.m., July 19th. The boy I was sure I was having turned out to be a little girl, Erin Lisa. She arrived July 20, 1965—11 days early.

HERE IT IS IN A NUTSHELL

There's a new Baby at our house!

Arrived 20 July, 1965
Weighing 6 lbs. 12¾ ozs.
Named Erin Lisa Mitchell

Jan at Tripler Army Hospital

Jimmy Becomes a Dad

"He often talked about his future child. We never really discussed the post Vietnam future because we knew there was a lot of time that had to pass before that happened. Jimmy always seemed to be waiting for me and would ask before I could even stop if I had heard anything about his baby. I remember showing up one evening with a smile on my face and his face immediately lit up because he knew I had some news to share. We sat on

some sandbags, and he said, "I guess I'm a dad," and I replied "yes." He lowered his head and looked at the ground for what seemed like several minutes. When he looked up, he had moist eyes and said what a great feeling it was. I looked away because I didn't think it would look too good to his and my men to see their Lieutenants crying together.

As I moved on to the next platoon, I could hear yells of joy from some of his Marines as the word began to spread through the lines.

Ed Howard
Former 1st Lieutenant
Delta Co. 1st Battalion
4th Marines
(Recollection in 1998)

Ed Howard and Jimmy

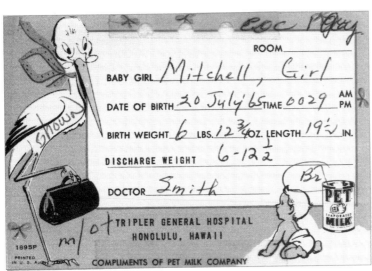

```
                              Headquarters
                      TRIPLER ARMY MEDICAL CENTER
                       APO San Francisco  96438


THPIO                                              3 Aug 65


Mrs. James M. Mitchell
430 North Kalaheo Ave.
Kailua, Oahu


Dear Mrs. Mitchell:

    We thought you might like to have a copy of the photograph that

was taken of you and your baby.

    It is an extra print of the one which was forwarded to your hus-

band by Tripler's commanding general, Major General W.D. Graham.


                                    Sincerely,



                                    JOHN SEEHAAS, DAC
                                    Public Information Officer
```

26 July 1965
Dear Wife and Mother, Big and Little Dog (Grandma & Grandpa),
Heard the wonderful news last night after returning from a very successful operation. I was just tickled to death. Can't really believe that I am the father of a 6 lb. 12½ oz. girl.
I received a letter from my mother, also, last night, upon return, informing me of the news. I only regret that I was not able to be with you but am so thankful that your parents were there. I hope you are fine honey, and that you didn't have too much trouble. I bet you are really relieved.

I just can't believe the good news. Please send me some pictures just as soon as you possibly can. Sure wish I could be with you all enjoying the excitement and thrills of being a parent. I guess I will just have to be content with being excited and thrilled out here in this hot box of sand.

I just saw Larry Faughn out in the field yesterday and told him it would probably be another five days before the big day. What a surprise. He has just returned from Oki. after spending a month there.

As I mentioned earlier our operation was quite successful. We moved up the coast a few miles and swept south down a peninsula with 2 companies while 1 company remained at the bottom as a blocking force. On our sweep we picked up 7 men hiding in small holes in the ground with grass and dirt over them. You almost had to step on them before you could detect them. They had no weapons but some of them are suspected as being V.C. One of them tried to run after we had caught him and as he ran he was shot in the foot which stopped his forward progress immediately. I will let you know how many V.C. we picked up as soon as I find out. Just about the time we got back home it really started to rain. This is really going to be some place when the rains begin. It just poured.

How does it feel to be a mother Janny, any different?? I can hardly wait to get home to be with my family. What a time we will have, French 75's and paper cut-out dolls, what a life.

Janet and Ernie,

How do you like our little place. I guess it hasn't changed much has it? What do you think of our new addition? I guess we will have to bring her up right, teach her to ski and enjoy warm weather early in life. I hope you both can stay as long as you desire there with Jan and I sure appreciate you both being there. You have made things a little easier on me. By the way you didn't get there any too soon. Wouldn't you know the bird would be early on something like that. She must have a weasel for a husband.

I sure miss you all and continually dream of all the good times we have had together. I bet we have had more fun than just about anyone.

Ernie and Janet, 1964

41

Please take good care of Janny and our little girl while I am gone. I am looking forward to the day we may all be together again. It won't be until after April or March I am sure. My first project is to finish my tour here in V.N. and will probably go to Oki for a few months and then to Southern California for duty, I hope.

Write soon and let me know how our little girl is getting along. We had better keep an eye on her, because if she takes after her mother and grandmother we are going to have our hands full.

Miss you all.
Love, Jim

27 July 1965

… I received the letter from Erin and really got a laugh out of it. I am keeping it with me and we will put it in our scrapbook later. … Am really looking forward to seeing some pictures of our little girl, happy she is so healthy. … On the 7th of August we will have been here three months. That doesn't sound like too long, but when you live the way we are living it's a long, long time. … Hi grandma and grandpa, what do you think of our little girl? Take good care of that little girl and her mother for me please. … I am so thrilled at being a father and when I read the letter from Erin, I had to hold the tears back. You know me, old sentimental Joe or is it Jimmy? …

28 July 1965
Dear Jan, Erin, Janet and Ernie,

I received your nice letters, Janet and Ernie, and needless to say was happy to hear from you and all about our little girl, Erin Lisa. Also enjoyed the pictures you enclosed. … Well, how's our little girl today, mother? I wish I could see her. I received a very cute card from JoAnn, Caryll and Sara, Jill and Jamy, Mary and Diane. Thank them all for me. … Janet, you mentioned in your letter it would have been nice if I could have been at the window when the baby was held up. I sure wish I could have been there also. What a thrill it would have been. Take real good care of that little girl, as I know without saying you all will. … I hope all is well with you, Jan, and that Erin is fine. Can hardly wait to get a picture.

Love Dad

42

Move Preparations

Upon my return from the hospital, my parents continued to stay with me and help with Erin. Finally, the day arrived when the movers came and packed the household goods. After the large moving truck left, we all began the chore of last-minute cleaning. When we finished, our dream house near the ocean sparkled. Even the green cement floors shined. I laughed and told my parents, "These floors are as shiny as Jimmy's military boots." I pointed to the small patio located off the living room and said, "That's where he spent a lot of his time—shining his boots and drinking iced tea. He'd be darn proud of these floors."

We had packed our suitcases earlier and were ready to leave. I took one last look around the house. I walked from room to room while I held Erin and then followed my mother and father out the kitchen door into the carport. The blue Corvair was waiting for us in the driveway. I felt more at ease knowing we had accomplished the tasks involved in a move. I also had feelings of sorrow. I knew I was giving up the house, the ocean, the outside carport parties and all the girlfriends that had become like close family. I knew Jimmy loved our time in Hawaii. It had been like a long honeymoon for both of us. I was leaving our house with its typical Hawaiian landscaping of palms, plumerias, hibiscus and coconut trees.

I backed out of the driveway for the last time. We left for Honolulu's International Airport. I saw my parents off and told them, "We'll be back to California once I get the car shipped and take care of a few more details on base." I headed back to Kailua to stay with my close friend, JoAnn. She too had a beautiful, new baby girl, Kimberly. Her husband was a 1st Lieutenant shipped out in early March along with the other 4,500 officers and men of the 1st Marine Brigade.

31 July 1965

... How's our little girl, honey? Is she walking yet or saying mommy and daddy? I sure wish I could be with you all. Send some pictures just as soon as you can and of the whole family along with some of Erin. ... I sure dream of the day when we can all be together again, and I can sit down and hold my little girl. For that matter, both of them ...

1 August Sunday, 9:00 a.m.

Well, I thought I would add some as I sit in my little house waiting for the truck to come by and pick us up for church call. I hope to go to communion and will say a few prayers for you all and ask that we may be together soon. ... It's going to be another hot one today. The water is already running off me. How is our little girl this morning?? Sure wish I could be with you all to enjoy the excitement of the new addition. It's going to be so nice to wake up in the morning and just lounge around the house all morning. ... Have you chosen any godparents Jan? How does the baby like her new room? Does she cry a lot? Are we going to have to keep her on a diet like her father should go on? ... How would you like a place on the beach or overlooking the cliff there in Leucadia? It may not be a good idea with Erin, however. It will also depend on where I am stationed—Camp Pendleton or MCRD ...

Love, Dad

6 August 1965

... I am just waiting for the day to see my little Erin. I just can't figure out where she got that little pug nose. ... In the next goodie box you send, how about smoked oysters, chili, popcorn, hard candy, shoe string potatoes and a kiss and hug from Erin and yourself. You will never know how much I love you—not until I return anyway. ... Take real good care of yourself and Erin, honey, and don't overdo a thing. Be real careful. ... It sounds as though Erin really keeps you on the go. How I wish I could be with you both. I hope and pray that all goes well over here and that we may be rejoined soon. ...

Love, Dad

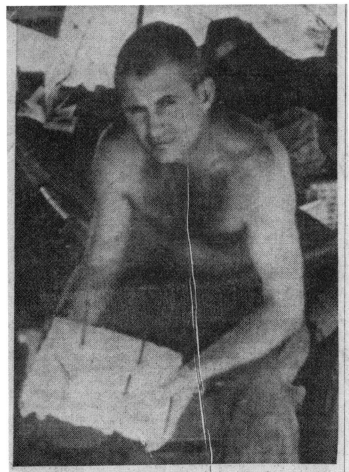

BATTLEFIELD BIRTHDAY CAKE—Some place in Vietnam, James M. Mitchell celebrated his 25th birthday August 8, just 23 days before his death. A cake-shaped block of mortar, studded with sharp spikes resembling those reported used by the Vietcong in booby traps, acted as his birthday cake, according to his widow.

8 August 1965

"… Can you imagine that 25 years have passed in my life? It seems strange to look back on those years. They have been happy ones, and I have been quite lucky …

10 August 1965, 12:00 Noon
Dear Jan and Erin,

I am sitting here waiting for General Westmoreland's arrival. How are my two girls? All is in good order I hope. I received a birthday card from my parents informing me that they were sending Erin a $50 bond. This will be placed toward her education. ... I sure miss you Janny and am beginning to think that it's going to be quite a while before we are again united. ... You are right about my birthday gift. You have presented me with the nicest gift anyone could ask for. I sure enjoyed the pictures you sent and am looking forward to many more. ... A couple of black and white pictures I snapped accidentally and don't know where the camera was pointing. I think it was pointed at my chest—Great huh!! ... From the sounds of things it seems as though that little girl is keeping you pretty busy honey. Don't over do it and get sick. I am grateful your folks were able to be with you. I know how much you have enjoyed having them there. ... Say, we are going to have to put that little girl on a diet, she already has a double chin like her old man. ... Who did she inherit that head of hair from? ... Sure wish I could be there to see my little girl. She looks so healthy. ... Will sign off now and enjoy the cute pictures of my family. ...

I Love You, Jimmy

— His Death —

Summers in Hawaii meant rain and heavy clouds hanging onto the lush towering mountains overlooking the town of Kailua. The town itself was bathed in sunlight. It also meant humidity, the fragrance of plumeria and a rainbow of pastels—the colors one associates with newborn babies.

What happened that August day is as clear to me now as it was 37 years ago. JoAnn and I were relishing our new roles as moms. Erin had just turned six weeks old and sported a full head of hair. There was no mistaking her for a boy. The ride from the base had put her fast asleep in the infant seat. She looked so small, fragile and tranquil, quite different from the past few weeks with her painful bouts of colic.

As we turned the corner to the house, we noticed a large, dark blue car parked along the street. Neither of us recognized the two men sitting in the car. We parked in the driveway and took our babies from the car, careful not to awaken either of them. I headed toward the trunk to grab a bag of items purchased from the base exchange. I recognized one of the men as he stepped out of the car. It was Lt. Colonel Edward Keyes Jr., the Brigade Comptroller and a long-time friend of Jimmy's family. When Jimmy's parents had come to the island the week he was shipped out, we had been invited to the Keyes' home for dinner, and it was there I met his wife, June, and their six-year-old daughter. Edward had visited our home several times to see how we were adjusting to our new life in the military. I was surprised to see him and greeted him with a smile and a wave. He did not acknowledge my greeting, but approached me quickly and purposefully. His face was somber, and he was turning his head from side to side. He seemed intent only on closing the distance between us.

Immediately sensing that something very serious had happened, my smile suddenly vanished into an expression of fear. I clutched the infant seat with trembling arms and dashed into the house followed by JoAnn and both men. My heart was racing. I took Erin directly to the bedroom and set her down on the rug in the plastic seat. Hurrying back to the living room, I was now faced with both men standing side by side. I glanced at the second man not knowing who he was. Edward immediately introduced him as the base chaplain stationed at Kaneohe Bay. Both men appeared uncomfortable in their situation.

"I have bad news, Jan."

Before Edward could utter another word, I asked, "Is he dead?"

"Yes," he replied. I put my hand to my forehead, thumb and middle finger pressing firmly to my temple and looked down. When I looked up, I felt as though I'd been hit by a sudden jolt of electricity followed by a total blank.

"No," I whispered. The chaplain walked nearer to me and said some words, probably of comfort I don't know. In despair I looked up at Edward and asked, "How was he killed?"

He replied, "a land mine." There was a pause, just long enough for the shock to radiate through my body.

"Are you sure he is really dead? Are you absolutely sure?"

His reply was, "Yes."

How could this be happening. God, this can't be true. This is impossible. Maybe he's been injured but not dead. "Are you *sure* he's dead?"

"Yes" was the reply. The finality was too difficult to comprehend. Edward then assured me that Jimmy's death had been confirmed before he came to the house. Silence. Taking short rapid breaths, I glanced at JoAnn. She appeared as stunned as I. The horror of war was suddenly a reality. What we thought could only happen to others and not us had happened. Within minutes, the course of my life had taken a different direction. I was 21 years old. Jimmy had just turned 25.

11 August 1965

... Jan, do you think I ought to teach Erin how to play basketball? You know you weren't too bad yourself. It's going to be so much fun watching her grow up. ... I sure miss my wife and daughter. The way the time is dragging on it seems as though it will be forever before we are united. ... By the way, I almost forgot I received a letter from my parents today. Guess what? They finally sold their house. I am so happy for them as it was so much work for both Dad and Mother. Now maybe they can get some much deserved rest and relaxation. I sure would like to see them also. Wouldn't you?? We are going to have such a good life once we are together again. I miss you so much it just can't be explained in words. ... How are the grandparents and aunts and uncles? I sure wish I

could be there to show off our little girl. Sounds as though she keeps you burning the midnight oil. … I sure am going to miss all the friends we have in Kailua, but get their addresses, and I am sure we will run into them again somewhere …

16 August 1965

… when you go home you stay wherever you wish, and if you want our furniture in the house, fine with me. I want you and Erin to be as comfortable and as happy as possible. … Have you had Erin baptized yet? I really enjoy the pictures you send of her and yourself. I look forward to a letter and a picture each day. … I love you honey and miss you so much. Just think how enjoyable it will be to be together again. How are grandma and grandpa? Hope they are having a good time and not spoiling that little girl, that's going to be my job. … Receiving two letters from you this afternoon did make me feel real good. I also enjoyed the picture of Erin and your mother. I sure get a thrill out of looking at that little girl. … I love and miss you Janny and our little Erin also. Please write often, your letters do wonders for me. …

My eyes turned to the chaplain. He suggested I sit. I plopped myself onto the sofa but not for long. There was no sitting still. I stood and started pacing not knowing exactly what to do with myself. I was aware of the silence in the house. All eyes were focused on me. The pacing continued and the question was asked once again not directing it to anyone in particular. "Are you SURE he's dead?" Almost in unison both men nodded and answered "Yes." How could I believe it? Jimmy Mitchell was indestructible. I looked at JoAnn who was now visibly shaken and mumbling for words to help. "I need a glass of water." I said, quivering. She hurried to the kitchen returning with the glass. I could tell she wanted to rescue me from the pain but there was no way to accomplish it. After taking several sips of the water, I handed it back.

Their message shocked me. I was intimidated by their rank, therefore, I tried to hide my emotions. I wanted to scream and pound my fists against the wall and sob, yet I couldn't draw a tear. I turned away and walked into the bedroom. Reaching down, I picked up Erin and carried her into the bathroom, and closed the door. No one tried to follow and disrupt my grief. Carefully setting my child down on a clothes hamper, I stood for a moment and stared at her. In a haze of unreality and feeling faint, I whispered, "God, God … oh, God …" I turned to the toilet and vomited.

```
[Mrs. Janet B. Mitchell              [COMPANY "D"
c/o Mrs. William C. G. Church        1st Battalion, 4th Marines (-) (Rein)
665 Ulumalu Street                   3rd Marine Division (Rein), FMF
Kailua, Oahu, Hawaii]                c/o FPO, San Francisco 96601
                                     1 September 1965]

UNCLAS
REQ YOU PASS THE FOLLOWING TO MRS JAMES M MITCHELL 665 ULUMAU KAILUA
OAHU HAWAII
QUOTE I DEEPLY REGRET TO CONFIRM THAT YOUR HUSBAND FIRST LIEUTENANT
JAMES M MITCHELL JR USMC DIED ON 31 AUGUST 75965 IN THE VICINITY OF CHU
LAI REPUNLIC OF VIETNAM FROM MULTIPLE FRAGMENTATION WOUNDS SUSTAINED
FROM AN UNKNOWN EXPLOSIVE DEVICE WHILE ON PATROL. HIS REMAINS
WILL BE PREPARED, ENCASED, AND SHIPPED AT NO EXPENSE TO YOU, ACCOMPANIED
BY AN ESCORT, EITHER TO A FUNERAL HOME OR TO A NATIONAL CEMETERY
SELECTED BY YOU. IN ADDITION YOU WILL BE REIMBURSED AN AMOUNT NOT TO
EXCEED TWO HUNDRED DOLLARS TOWARD FUNERAL AND INTERMENT EXPENSES IF


PAGE TWO RUECEM 11 UNCLAS
INTERMENT IS IN A PRIVATE CEMETERY, ONE HUNDRED TWENTY-FIVE DOLLARS
IF REMAINS ARE CONSIGNED TO A FUNERAL HOME PRIOR TO INTERMENT IN A
NATIONAL CEMETERY, OR SEVENTY-FIVE DOLLARS IF REMAINS ARE CONSIGNED
DIRECTLY TO A NATIONAL CEMETERY. PLEASE WIRE COLLECT HEADQUARTERS
MARINE CORPS YOUR DESIRES IN THIYICJLOENJ, INDICATING THE NAME AND
ADDRESS OF THE FUNERAL HOME OR NATIONAL CEMETERY TO WHICH YOU WISH
THE REMAINS SENT AND WHETHER OR NOT YOU DESIRE AN ESCORT. THE
NATIONAL MEMORIAL CEMETERY OF THE PACIFIC HONOLULU HAWAII IS NEAREST
YOUR HOME. LETTER WILL FOLLOW CONCERNING CIRCUMSTANCES OF DEATH. I
WISH TO ASSURE YOU OF EVERY POSSIBLE ASSISTANCE AND TO EXTEND THE
HEARTFELT CONDOLENCES OF THE MARINE CORPS IN YOUR BEREAVEMENT. UNQUOTE
WALLACE M GREENE NR GENERAL USMC COMMANDANT OF THE MARINE CORPS
BT
COPIES TO MARBRIG
TOR:01/07562/SEPT65/B/RC/#0049                            0101452
G-1-2-3-4 ADJ CEO COMPT MED        LEG ISO S&C SS MT DISBO AIR
```

20 August 1965

... Things are about the same here, not too much new. Still working rather long hours, not much sleep to be had by anyone ... Will be happy when I can go to bed at night without a pistol on my chest ... Yes, I have had my platoon for quite some time now, but don't know as I would be happy with anything else. Only time will tell I guess ... Please write often as I sure enjoy hearing from you and to receive all the news of Erin and what she is up to ... It's only a matter of time honey and we will again be together.

Love, Jimmy

23 August 1965

Dear Jan and Erin,

Received your letter dated 16 August with the clippings. Enjoyed reading them. I bet you are getting excited about your move. Sure would like to be there to give you a hand and to accompany you and our little daughter back home. My folks are really looking forward to seeing you and Erin ... If you can, try and send a picture with each letter as I really look forward to receiving both your letter and a picture. You should be receiving or should have received the 3 rolls of film I sent you. Hope you enjoy them. They will mean a lot to us when we are home together ... Well honey, it won't be long now and you will be headed for home. Don't get overly tired and overdo it. Take it real slow and easy and whatever you do, don't cut that little doll's hair. By the time I get home she should have a nice long ponytail. If my wife won't grow a ponytail for me, maybe my daughter will??? ... Yes, just about all I can think about is our next little house overlooking the ocean from the cliffs in Leucadia or Encinitas. There will be so many enjoyable evenings spent together just relaxing enjoying each other's company, our little girl, music, and a cold drink. You can't imagine how much one appreciates the small things in life. I love you so much and am praying that we will soon be able to return to a normal life ... When you drive the car with Erin, don't pay a bit of attention to her while you are driving because if you should look at her you may run into something. You may recall I ran off the road one time while watching our little dog in Rancho. Please write soon Janny and take it easy during the move.

I Love You Honey, Jimmy

JoAnn knocked on the door after giving me a few moments alone. We walked to the living room. "Jan, we need you to pack your things and come with us as soon as you can." Edward spoke compassionately but with authority. Remembering exactly what I was wearing — khaki Bermudas with a rust and blue short-sleeved Chinese collared shirt — I gathered what things I had. In what seemed like seconds we were in the blue car. I never exchanged good-byes with JoAnn.

The only sound in the car was the fan blowing. I stared out the window and watched the palm trees race past us in a blur. When we arrived on base, we took the chaplain to his office. "You and Erin will be staying with June and I tonight. I've made reservations for you on United tomorrow morning." I gave a slight nod, and we continued on.

June opened the front door when she heard our car approach the house. She had an unsettled look on her face but said nothing. She quickly escorted us to the second floor where we would be staying in her six-year old daughter's room. Like any curious six-year-old, Shirley Ann peeked at me from around the corner, stared for a moment with a bewildered look and left. The bed in Shirley's room was white with a canopy. Setting my little girl down, I tried to gather my thoughts. My priority was contacting her pediatrician. She had suffered several bouts of severe colic and Dr. Stephenson had put her on a special formula. At the moment she was sleeping soundly.

Edward came upstairs. "Jan, I really want you with me when I call Peter and Luella, can you come down to the kitchen while I call?" So that was the rush, I thought … my God they don't know yet! I followed Edward downstairs and sat very still as he made the long distance call. I listened as he delivered the news … "Peter," he said, "this is Edward." Whatever Peter's response was, Edward replied, "He's dead." The conversation was abrupt. After the call, I went back to the white canopied bed. Still concerned about Erin, I called her pediatrician thinking he would be home from his office. His wife answered and I explained with some difficulty what had happened. She promised to give him my message the minute he arrived.

It was nearing sunset, and June suggested we take a walk near the ocean. I didn't want to. I didn't want to do anything but think … to think about my husband. I needed to try and comprehend what had happened. Everything taking place around me was like a movie sped up in fast motion. She tried to make conversation, but I didn't hear her words. I looked out to the ocean while the tears rolled down my face, and the shredded tissue continued to soak up what it could. It was a short walk. She knew.

Soon after we returned to the house, Dr. Stephenson called. It was a professional call with his attention focused only on my child's care. He gave me the medical information needed, lots of reassurance, and his condolences.

24 August 1965, 10:00 A.M.

… by the time you are reading this you should be living with JoAnn … I love you honey. I am getting to the point that all I can think about is the three of us getting back together and living in our little dream house … Would you send me some more envelopes when you can? Don't put any stamps on them as soon, we will be able to send letters from here without postage. I also see that we will be getting a pay raise and our combat pay has been increased $10. All of this does not bring us together which I hope will be the next step. I miss you so much honey. It seems as though we have been apart a year or two and here it has only been about 6 months. It seems as though I have been in Vietnam 2 years. What a place this is. It's really not too bad except for the terrible heat. Take real good care of yourself honey and Erin. I sure miss you both and pray that soon we will be united … Be sure and drive carefully when you return to California … I love you Janny. Send a picture as often as you can.

Love to my wife and daughter, Jimmy

Encinitas, California, August 31, 1965

The phone rang at 1183 Saxony Road. "Hello," my mother answered.

"Janet?"

"Yes" she responded.

"This is Peter. Are you alone or is Ernie with you?"

"I'm alone" she replied. "Ernie is at my brother's house."

"Janet … James has been killed." So startled, she pulled the receiver slightly away from her ear and gasped. She could hear Peter say, "She's taking it very hard." My mother couldn't talk. After hanging up, she called her brother's house. My Aunt Jean answered the phone. My mother told her what happened. She turned to my father and said, "Ernie, Jimmy's been injured." My father was out the door in seconds. He arrived home to find his wife standing in the living room with swollen eyes, obviously shaken.

"What's happened to Jimmy?" my dad asked.

"Ernie," her voice quavering, "Jimmy's dead."

He walked into the kitchen and kicked a hole in one of the cabinets.

Kaneohe Bay, Hawaii, August 31, 1965

Shortly after I spoke with the pediatrician, my mother called from Encinitas. "Jan, are you and the baby okay?" Her voice had a nasal tone like someone suffering from a cold or allergies. "Peter just phoned us a while ago and gave us the terrible news. Daddy's sick—we're just sick."

"Yes, we're okay," I replied. "This is all so awful," I wept. "Does anyone else know what's happened yet?"

"Almost everyone in town. The word has spread fast. I was still unpacking our things when Peter called," she said.

I told her I would be home the next day. We had an early morning flight. "Please don't talk about anything that's happened when you and his parents pick us up at the airport, okay?" "Please," I emphasized somewhat sternly, "we've gotta hold up. It's what Jimmy would want." I started to fret.

How will I act, like nothing happened? Should I keep the conversation focused on Erin? Oh, how I dread this reunion—so different from the fun we had together in March. How am I going to face the mother and stepfather who adored their only child?

That night, my five closest girlfriends came by. JoAnn and I hugged. There was an awkwardness and uneasy silence. Speaking up to ease the strain I said, "I know none of you know what to say. Just sit down."

Everyone knew the minute they entered the room that few words would be consoling. My friend Mary was employed on the other side of the mountain known as the Pali. She was a secretary at Camp Smith in the office of the Commander of Chief, Pacific Forces. From her, our group of girls got bits of information—the latest scoop related to our husbands. Mary had heard the news on the radio while driving home from work. She became frantic as she raced home to tell her roommate, Jill. JoAnn had already called and informed Jill of the news, along with Caryll. Jill, in turn, called Diane.

Keeping her composure, Jill spoke in her Texas accent. "I have some news I want to give ya, darlin. Can you please come right over?" When Diane arrived, Caryll was already with Jill. While they broke the news to Diane, Mary drove into the driveway and sprang from her car. She dashed into the house—wild with emotion.

Mary sat in a chair across from the other girls who were seated on the sofa. She came to me and recited a poignant poem about a soldier dying in battle. She had seen it in a magazine and memorized it months before Jimmy's death. She was deeply moved by the poem and recited it to me as she knelt on her knees. (A few years later, she would be looking for the poem she had memorized, but had since forgotten. She wanted to recite it at her younger brother's funeral. He was also killed in Vietnam.)

I went to Caryll because she was a very religious person. I needed reassurance from someone like her. I wanted to hear that Jimmy was okay. "Jan, the good man that he was, he is most likely with God." We sat together on the white bed and cried and cried and cried.

The day had taken its toll. Everyone was exhausted. June and I walked my friends to the door. I continued to follow them out to the car and thanked them for coming.

Darkness and the electric clock with its soft rhythmic buzz; no other sounds in the room. Drained of all energy, but unable to sleep, I crept into June and Edward's bedroom. They had taken Erin, thinking it would be of help to me. I felt uneasy, almost panicky. I knelt over the borrowed bassinet to find her asleep. I returned to my room and began pacing. The "Committee" that we all have when things go wrong had gathered in my head, and the session was about to commence. Feelings of guilt took over.

I should have gone to church more. If I could just have back the times we had silly spats. If I could have back _any_ time. "Jesus help me," I whispered. Falling on the bed, I sobbed.

Shortly thereafter I went back to Erin's side—always keeping vigil over her. The dark night and the pacing continued until the Committee closed session at dawn.

Kaneohe Bay, Hawaii, September 1, 1965

The clock read 5 a.m. I went to Erin's side and carried her back to the white canopied bed. Holding her snuggly while she took her morning bottle, I felt some comfort that I was holding a part of her dad.

I dressed her in a tiny pink terrycloth jump suit. Her colic had subsided, and she sat contentedly in her seat, eyes gazing inquisitively at her surroundings. She resembled her father a great deal, and I would find myself haunted with the thought he would never see her.

I dressed myself, but in slow motion. Everything I picked up felt heavy, even the hair brush. When we were ready to leave, the final glimpse in the mirror showed me that in less than 24 hours I looked 10 years older.

Edward drove us to the airport. The girls were waiting for our arrival. There were more tears and more embraces. The shock of the news of Jimmy's death had sunk in. Someone handed me the Honolulu Advertiser. I looked at the front page. EX-ISLE MARINE KILLED. The article reported what I already knew.

Edward accompanied us outside to the United Airlines DC8. We walked up the portable staircase to the aircraft. He made sure we were seated and said goodbye. In nine days we would meet again.

Midway into the flight I began to feel queasy. I had a window seat, and Erin sat next to me in her infant seat in the middle section. The aisle seat was occupied by a lady I remember as in her mid 30s. My baby needed her diaper changed, but gradually my queasiness turned to nausea and dizziness. I bent forward and slightly tapped her on the leg. "I'm sorry," I whispered. "Could you please help me with my baby? She needs her diaper changed, and I need to use the restroom. My husband was killed in Vietnam yesterday, and we're going home." She instinctively took charge of Erin and cared for her the rest of the flight. I made my way down the aisle grabbing the back of each seat as I wavered from side to side. The stares from passengers had no affect on me. The walk seemed to take forever.

When I returned to my seat, the lady was holding Erin and gently patting her back. She said, "Try and get some sleep. I'll take care of the baby. She'll be okay. Don't worry about her." Hearing those words, I fell into a deep sleep.

We landed at Los Angeles International Airport. United personnel were there to escort us to a private area. Thanking the lady several times, I climbed aboard the small commuter car. She didn't speak. She stood watching, and we disappeared into the crowd.

We had a two-hour layover in Los Angeles. A United Airlines employee sat with us in the small room. I brought out pictures of Jimmy in Chu Lai and explained what happened. I also showed her pictures of Erin. She gave a half smile—a kind of sickening regretful smile. I started to cry.

Three hours later we were in San Diego; we were home.

The stewardess told me to stay seated until all the passengers had departed. The first and only person to come aboard was my father. "Hi Janny. Let me help you with 'Soupy,' as he had nicknamed her in Hawaii."

He carried Erin off the plane, and I followed. Both grandmothers were standing in the terminal. Peter stood in the distance. As I had requested on the phone to my mother, there was no drama—no outward grief. Jimmy's mom took her granddaughter in her arms and held her close for the first time. I could almost see the pain in her heart. Peter walked over and suggested we go to the car. It was difficult to face him. I guessed at his thoughts. My mother fussed over Erin, dressed in her pink jumpsuit, somehow trying to distract the signs of tragedy. We left for the ride to Encinitas.

Like other events leading to the flight home, there was silence. The scenes repeated themselves. No one knew what to say. The pain endured within us—we all had our own thoughts. Like myself, Luella continued to hold the baby snuggly as if she too were getting some relief by holding a part of her son.

27 August, 1965, 6:00 P.M.
Dear wife and daughter,

I love you both. How's that for a good beginning. I haven't received any mail for four days, neither has anyone else. This mail service leaves a great deal to be desired. There are two things I look forward to each day. One is to see the 2 cans of beer a man brings over the desert. The other thing is to see the man carrying the mail sack trudging through the sand … How is that little girl of ours? Is she being good? Does she still keep you awake all night? … How did the move go? … Is Erin growing fast? Is her hair getting any lighter? Have you put her on a diet yet? … I stopped to count how long I have been a platoon commander and was quite surprised when I came up with 15 months. That is quite a while to be with one unit … I dream each day of the time when we are back together again just sitting across the table from each other making funny faces. Only now there will be someone in between us to give us a little more pleasure. I can hardly wait to see our little Erin. I love you both so much … No mail as yet so will close and hope for tomorrow. I love you and Erin and miss you.

Love, Jimmy

When we reached my parents' house, I went to the bedroom and undressed as slowly as I had dressed before leaving Hawaii. My mother took over. Once again, Erin was placed in a borrowed bassinet. She took her to their bedroom. She and my father knew exactly how to care for her since they were there for Erin's first days in Hawaii. I crawled into bed. Luella and Peter drove home.

People came; people went. I couldn't eat; I couldn't visit. I only wanted to sleep.

When my head cleared I thought about funeral arrangements. I was told

Peter was handling them. In spite of his own pain, he continued to take charge. He made sure everything was handled properly.

On the 7th, my mother drove the baby and me to the pediatrician's office in Oceanside. When I was 19, I had worked there. Erin needed a six-week checkup. It was the same scenario—the tragedy was not discussed, and the friends I had worked with kept their distance. She saw Dr. Ward and weighed in at 8 lbs. 14 oz. The nurse gave her vaccines, Donnatal for her colic and made us a return appointment in one month.

That evening the telegrams began to arrive.

SEP
1
A.M.
1965

WESTERN UNION
TELEGRAM
1201 (4-60)

CLASS OF SERVICE
This is a fast message
unless its deferred char-
acter is indicated by the
proper symbol.

SYMBOLS
DL = Day Letter
NL = Night Letter
LT = International
Letter Telegram

W. P. MARSHALL, PRESIDENT

The filing time shown in the date line on domestic telegrams is LOCAL TIME at point of origin. Time of receipt is LOCAL TIME at point of destination

WUAO 41

SY WB280 XV GOVT PD=FAX WASHINGTON DC 7 634P EDT=

=MRS JAMES M MITCHELL, CARE E A BERTONCINI=

1183 SAXONY ST ENCINITAS CALIF

=THE REMAINS OF YOUR HUSBAND FIRST LIEUTENANT

JAMES M MITCHELL JR ARE BEING RETURNED FROM VIETNAM BY

AIR AND WILL BE TRANSPORTED VIA THE MOST EXPEDITIOUS MEANS

FROM SAN FRANCISCO CALIF TO SAN DIEGO CALIF. I AM AWARE

OF THE PRESSING DESIRE FOR THE RETURN OF HIS REMAINS AND

EVERY EFFORT WILL BE MADE TO EXPEDITE SHIPMENT.

THE COMPANY WILL APPRECIATE SUGGESTIONS FROM ITS PATRONS CONCERNING ITS SERVICE

WESTERN UNION
TELEGRAM
1201 (4-60)

CLASS OF SERVICE
This is a fast message
unless its deferred char-
acter is indicated by the
proper symbol.

SYMBOLS
DL = Day Letter
NL = Night Letter
LT = International
Letter Telegram

W. P. MARSHALL, PRESIDENT

The filing time shown in the date line on domestic telegrams is LOCAL TIME at point of origin. Time of receipt is LOCAL TIME at point of destination

IT IS SUGGESTED THAT YOU DELAY SCHEDULING FUNERAL SERVICES

UNTIL YOU AND SUPT FORT ROSECRANS NATIONAL CEMETERY ARE

NOTIFIED BY THE COMMANDING OFFICER NAVAL DISPENSARY

SAN FRANCISCO CALIF OF THE EXPECTED TIME AND DATE OF

ARRIVAL OF REMAINS IN SAN DIEGO CALIF. PLEASE BE ASSURED

OF MY CONTINUED SYMPATHY=

=WALLACE M GREENE JR

GENERAL USMC COMMANDANT OF THE MARINE CORPS=

THE COMPANY WILL APPRECIATE SUGGESTIONS FROM ITS PATRONS CONCERNING ITS SERVICE

WESTERN UNION
TELEGRAM
W. P. MARSHALL, PRESIDENT

Class of Service: This is a fast message unless its deferred character is indicated by the proper symbol.

SYMBOLS
DL=Day Letter
NL=Night Letter
LT=International Letter Telegram

The filing time shown in the date line on domestic telegrams is LOCAL TIME at point of origin. Time of receipt is LOCAL TIME at point of destination

WU0 39

L LLG460 XV GOVT PD 2 EXTRA=TDL PWS SAN FRANCISCO CALIF

SEPT 7 1039P PDT=

CRE MR E A BERTONCINI

1183 SAXONY ST ENCINITAS CALIF=

INFO FOR BUMED CMC COMTWELVE COMELEVEN DIRTWELTHMARCORDIST

CG MARCOPCRUITDEP SDIEGO SUPT FORT ROSECRANS NATCE

M SDIEGO MARBKS NAV TI REMAINS OF YOUR HUSBAND 1ST

LT JAMES N MITCHELL JR 087976 USMC ARRIVED IN SAN FRANCISCO

CALIF AT 3:30PM 7 SEPT 1965. REGRET THAT NECESSARY MORTUARY

SERVICES HERE WILL CAUSE SLIGHT ADDITIONAL DELAY.

THE COMPANY WILL APPRECIATE SUGGESTIONS FROM ITS PATRONS CONCERNING ITS SERVICE

WESTERN UNION
TELEGRAM
W. P. MARSHALL, PRESIDENT

Class of Service: This is a fast message unless its deferred character is indicated by the proper symbol.

SYMBOLS
DL=Day Letter
NL=Night Letter
LT=International Letter Telegram

The filing time shown in the date line on domestic telegrams is LOCAL TIME at point of origin. Time of receipt is LOCAL TIME at point of destination

VIEWING LEFT TO DISCRETION OF FUNERAL DIRECTOR.

FEATHERINGILL MORTUARY SAN DIEGO CALIF HAS BEEN REQUESTED

TO MEET PLANE. ESCORT LT COL EDWARD B KEYES JR USMC WILL

ACCOMPANY THE REMAINS. COMMANDING OFFICER US NAVAL DISPENSARY

SAN FRANCISCO CALIF=

NAVAL DISPENSARY 091932Z ==

THE COMPANY WILL APPRECIATE SUGGESTIONS FROM ITS PATRONS CONCERNING ITS SERVICE

SEP 1 A.M. 1965

8¢ U.S. AIR MAIL

WESTERN UNION TELEGRAM

CLASS OF SERVICE
This is a fast message unless its deferred character is indicated by the proper symbol.

W. P. MARSHALL, PRESIDENT

1201 (4-60)

SYMBOLS
DL = Day Letter
NL = Night Letter
LT = International Letter Telegram

The filing time shown in the date line on domestic telegrams is LOCAL TIME at point of origin. Time of receipt is LOCAL TIME at point of destination

= | =WUO 38

LLHO95 GOVT PRIORITY PD=TDL PWS SAN FRANCISCO 9 228P PDT

=MRS JANET B MITCHELL CARE E A BERTONCINI DO NOT FWD=

: 1183 SAXONY ST ENCINITAS CALIF:

=ACTION FOR MRS JANET B MITCHEL, INFO FOR MRS LUELLA M

MCCONALD 1675 CREST DRIVE ENCINITAS CALIF, MR JAMES MITCHELL

1170 9TH ST ALAMEDA CALIF REMAINS OF YOUR HUSBAND

1ST LT JAMES M MITCHELL USMC WILL DEPART SAN FRANCISCO CALIF

VIA COMMERCIAL AIR AT 5:40 PM 9 SEPT 1965 ON UNITED AIR

LINES FLT 521 TO ARRIVE SAN DIEGO CALIF /AT 654 PM 9 SEPT

1965.

THE COMPANY WILL APPRECIATE SUGGESTIONS FROM ITS PATRONS CONCERNING ITS SERVICE

WESTERN UNION TELEGRAM

CLASS OF SERVICE
This is a fast message unless its deferred character is indicated by the proper symbol.

W. P. MARSHALL, PRESIDENT

1201 (4-60)

SYMBOLS
DL = Day Letter
NL = Night Letter
LT = International Letter Telegram

The filing time shown in the date line on domestic telegrams is LOCAL TIME at point of origin. Time of receipt is LOCAL TIME at point of destination

YOU WILL BE INFORMED OF TRNSPORATION TO SAN DIEGO CALIF

AT THE EARLIEST POSSIBLE TIME. SINCEREST SYMPATHY EXTENDED.

COMMANDING OFFICERUS NAVAL DISPENSARY SAN FRANCISCO CALIF

= NAVAL DISPENSARY 080049"=

THE COMPANY WILL APPRECIATE SUGGESTIONS FROM ITS PATRONS CONCERNING ITS SERVICE

28 August 1965, 6:00 P.M.

Dear Jan and Erin,

I received a wonderful letter from you today honey. The first I might add in 5 days. To answer one question, yes, I think B.J. and Caryll will be the best godparents for our little girl … It sounds as though the only thing that little girl does is eat. You had better put her on a diet or she will look like her dad … All I can think about is the three of us together. I know these letters sound like a stuck record as I say the same thing over and over again — like I love you … I am planning to ask B.J. tomorrow at church if they would be godparents for Erin. I will probably not get this letter off until tomorrow so will tell you his answer later in the letter … Sunday morning 9:30 A.M. 29 August. Well here I am again back in my house. Had a sleepless night, about 2 hours. I am waiting this morning in hopes a truck will come by to take us to mass. It doesn't look as though it will show. I also wanted to talk with Brian about Erin but I guess that will have to wait. I hope that today we get a lot of mail as it has been a long time since any mail to speak of has arrived … How is our little girl today? I sure wish I could be with you all. Remember how enjoyable our Sundays used to be? Just a relaxing day after church, popcorn, the beach and a Sunday afternoon nap. Oh well, one of these days we will be repeating the same thing only in good old Southern California … Won't it be nice, only about 7 months to go … It is now 12:30 P.M. and I am waiting for both the mail and the beer to come down the hill … I love you honey. How was your trip back to California? Hope an enjoyable one and not too tiring. The mail is really screwed up again. Only two letters came down for the platoon and I was not one of the lucky ones. I am still hoping for later tonight … How do you like being back in Southern California and Encinitas? Has the place changed much? I am looking forward to being home … 1:45 P.M. Well, one of my daily wishes has come true. Just received my daily ration of 2 beers. Have lighted up a cigar so will just sit back and dream of my wife and daughter … 6:10 P.M. Have had chow, briefed the squad leaders for the night so am ready for another night. Over in the hills it looks as though it may rain. Hope not as it can really be miserable … I love you bird and continually think of the day when we again will be together. What a happy day it will be. If the day were tomorrow it wouldn't be soon enough.

By the way it doesn't look as though we will be getting anymore mail tonight. Maybe tomorrow! Write soon and please say hello to your folks and mine when you see them.

Love, Jimmy

I had never received a telegram. The word "remains" sounded hideous and caught me off guard. My expression must have revealed my shock.

"Jan, I know what you're feeling," my dad said. "Are you wondering what remains means?" he asked.

"Yes," I said with a deep sigh, "and why are the mortuary services being delayed?"

He walked away from me while turning his head around. "I don't know why they are delayed." He stopped for a moment. "Remains is a term used for a deceased body. It doesn't necessarily mean he was blown up." He solemnly continued his walk to the bedroom where he and my mother watched over Erin.

Jimmy's remains arrived on the 9th, escorted by Lt. Col. Edward B. Keyes Jr., the man who initially told me of Jimmy's death.

Hard Reality

The following morning Peter and Luella arrived at the house. We drove to the mortuary. The three of us stood outside the room where the body lay. Peter told me to go in first, and they would wait their turn. I walked in and closed the door. I knelt by the silver casket in silence for a brief moment. I stood up and walked around the casket staring at it. I rubbed my hand across the top of the cold metal box. I tried to visualize what he looked like. He was dressed in Marine Corps "Dress Blues." Laying my head on top of the casket I whispered to him. I whispered everything to him about his baby. I whispered over and over and over how much I loved him. Tears flowed down the sides of my face onto the box and a deep moan emerged from a part of my gut.

That evening, Luella's eldest sister Audrey arrived from the state of Washington. Erin and I went to meet her at Jimmy's folks. There was an abundance of food from friends and family. The five of us sat down for dinner. The conversation was light and relaxed. The attention was on Erin. I held her as I ate, and, for a brief moment, I had a feeling of relief and peace as I watched Luella enjoying the dinner. In seconds, that changed. She dropped her fork. Covering her face with a napkin, she kept repeating, "James isn't here—he'll never be with us again …" The dinner ended shortly thereafter.

The night before the funeral, Jimmy's dad arrived with his wife Betty and Jimmy's stepbrothers, John, 12, and Leo, 10.

The funeral was held September 13th.

The church was packed. I sat in the front row on the right side next to John and Leo. The silver metal casket draped with the U.S. flag was placed in front of the alter. *I wonder what he looks like? Would there be bruises and cuts on his face? Where did they get his dress blues? Do they put shoes on corpses? Someone told me once they didn't.*

The mass began and throughout the service, tears of grief fell as the boys and I went together to receive communion. John, number two son as Jimmy Sr. called him, felt the loss deeply. The 12-year-old's sobs filled the church. When the funeral mass ended, I followed the casket out of the church, down the church stairs—the same stairs I walked down arm-in-arm with my new husband 17 months earlier.

SAN DIEGO UNION

Dream Dies For Their 'Good Life'

Marine's Hopes End in Vietnam Combat Patrol

"We are going to have such a good life," wrote Marine Lt. James Mitchell, "once we are together again.

"If you only knew how much I want to see our little girl ... "

The letter came from Vietnam. The words were for his wife, Jan, who waited for him in Hawaii. He never came back.

James Mitchell, 25, was killed Tuesday on combat patrol in Chu Lai.

NEVER SAW DAUGHTER

He was never to see that little girl. Erin Lisa Mitchell was born in July. Her father went to Vietnam in May.

Twenty-five years is very young. It is old enough to know the horrors of war. But it is young enough to hope and to dream.

"I pray for the day that we will join each other," he wrote his wife. "I hope it will come soon and without incident."

Jan Mitchell, a widow at 21, was a Marine wife through and through. Still, it is hard to understand. In those letters there is small measure of solace.

LIFE IN VIETNAM

This, in Lt. James Mitchell's words, is Vietnam.

"Still working long hours. No sleep without a pistol on my chest ...

"One of the men was injured by a booby trap. They are worse than running into 20 Viet Cong. You don't know where they are and then, all of a sudden, boom! ...

"There were quite a few Viet Cong in the area today. Got sniped at a number of times. Returned fire, no bodies, but a number of blood stains. One just can't see the enemy. They are real well hidden ...

"The heat is unbearable. We spent a miserable, wet night last night. We patrolled until 2:30 a.m. and then were eaten by mosquitoes and shook to death the rest of the night ... "

PARENT'S HOME

She thumbed through the letters at the home of her parents, Mr. and Mrs. Ernest Bertoncini of Encinitas, where she and Erin Lisa will be staying for a while.

The memories are painful. There were the school days together at San Dieguito Union High, where James Mitchell was the 1959 student body president and the most popular boy in the class.

There was the wedding here in April 1964. There is the home in Encinitas where his mother and stepfather, retired Marine Colonel and Mrs. Peter A. McDonald live.

James Mitchell, the boy who had everything going for him, is dead in a war that is only half a war.

Oceanside Tribune
Irv Grossman
Sept '65

GROSSMAN

Jimmy Mitchell

There was hardly anything to him. I mean, he was a shade over five feet, and he long since had quit growing. When he bent over, his mother could lose him in a cabbage patch.

But he was an athlete and a scholar and a popular kid in every way. It all came out of him—the ability, the desire, the great striving—every minute of his waking life like glue from a punctured tube.

Jimmy Mitchell is dead now, killed last week in Vietnam. His mourners are many.

You may not remember the name but you may recall the face. He was blonde and blue-eyed with a kewpie-like face. Always he was quick and alert, moving like a little puppy that is attracted to a bone. He was so fast that a rumor would have trouble keeping up with him.

He came out of Encinitas and played for San Dieguito High School. He was a halfback who caught the winning touchdown pass when San Dieguito defeated Oceanside in 1959. He was the guard in basketball who dribbled past the Oceanside press and the dash man in track who ran away with the league meet.

Jimmy Mitchell was a little man who played sports like a giant.

Suffering Each Defeat

Don Huffman, Oceanside basketball coach, believes Mitchell was the best defensive high school basketball player this area ever produced.

"Defensively, no one was his equal," Huffman said. "And he was an expert dribbler. He could break a full court press by himself. "

"But I'll always remember Mitchell most for his competitive spirit. There has never been a high school athlete who wanted to win as badly as he did."

There was a game in 1959 between Oceanside and San Dieguito and the result meant little. Neither school claimed a championship basketball team and neither would improve its position in the standings with a victory. Oceanside won and Mitchell cried.

"He suffered with the defeat," Huffman recalled.

You know how little guys are in sports. They get the razz. All the audiences were hostile towards Mitchell, but the kid handled such abuse with dignity and courage. And when the game was over, his tormentors most often then wished that Mitchell had been playing for their side.

"I know the Oceanside players detested Mitchell when they played against him," Huffman said. "But they sure would have liked it if he were playing for them."

Basketball was his great love, and he went on to captain a championship Palomar College team in 1960-61.

"He was the club's rally man," recalled Palomar coach Joe Brennan. "When the team needed the spectacular play to get it going, Mitchell would come up with it."

He arrived at Palomar armed with all the necessary defensive technique and ball handling ability, but he lacked a consistent scoring touch.

"Mitchell was the first one on the court and the last off it," Brennan said. "He realized what he had to learn, and he worked as hard as he could to improve himself."

Wanted to Be a Coach

He realized that his size often turned against him. But instead of brooding because he wasn't the beneficiary of an anthropologist's blessing, Mitchell accepted his lack of height as a challenge.

"It was his way never to stop learning," Brennan said, "No matter whether we won or lost, he wanted to know what he had done wrong."

Possibly, it was such an attitude that allowed him to be an honor student, an officer of his class and one of the most popular persons ever to attend San Dieguito.

"He won the respect of all classes of people," said Sam McCracken of the high school. "The bad kids as well as the good kids liked him. So did the adults. And it all came naturally to him."

He had hoped to return to this area after Vietnam. He had qualified for his teacher's credential and wanted to be a coach.

"Jimmy would have made a terrific coach," McCracken said. "He loved kids as much as he loved athletics."

You hear about the high cost of the war in Vietnam and every day another set of casualty figures is released. The digits mean something and then they don't—unless one of them is a face.

So they will bring the body of Jimmy Mitchell home and there will be military graveside services at Fort Rosecrans National Cemetery. We grieve for his wife and his child and his parents. And we want them to know that Jimmy Mitchell will reside in the memories of many people in this area for many years to come.

PALOMAR COLLEGE

PHONE 744-1150   PHONE 727-7529

SAN MARCOS, CALIFORNIA 92069

September 10, 1965

Mrs. James Mitchell
c/o 220-1/2 10th
Del Mar, California

Dear Mrs. Mitchell:

On behalf of Palomar College, I wish to express the very deep regret and sympathy of the faculty and the students for the death of your husband. As I am sure you know, he was held in great esteem and also with much affection by all who knew him. I did not have the pleasure of knowing Jim; however, I have learned a great deal about him in the past few days from those who did.

On September 17th, at 10:00 a.m., we are holding our annual Convocation on the college campus, and as a part of our program, there will be a brief memorial service for your husband. We would be pleased and honored if you would be able to attend. Mr. Joe Brennan will be contacting you by telephone within a few days.

If there is anything at all that I, personally, or the college can do, please let me know.

Sincerely yours,

Fred Huber

Frederick R. Huber
President

MEMORIAL PLAQUE DEDICATED

The widow and parents of Lt. James Mitchell stand before memorial plaque dedicated yesterday at Palomar College in honor of former students killed in Viet Nam. From left are Mrs. Jean Mitchell, Col. John McDonald, USMC, ret., and Mrs. McDonald. Mitchell, a former Palomar basketball star, was killed in action with the Marine Corps in Viet Nam.

68

Fellow Officer in Viet Nam Lauds Encinitas War Hero

Editor: I received an article taken from the Evening Tribune concerning a memorial plaque inscribed with the name of 1st Lt. James M. Mitchell, USMC. It was sent to me by his wife, and I thank you and her for giving me the opportunity to read it.

I had known Jim Mitchell only since he joined the 1st Marine Brigade in Hawaii in early 1964. We were both platoon commanders in Company D at the time. We served here in Viet Nam together, in the same battalion, until the day he died.

Jim has been given a fine tribute with that plaque, and I would like to commend you for your article, and Palomar College for the dedication of the plaque and the significant thought behind it.

A few weeks ago I read an article, from the Encinitas Coast Dispatch, I believe, stating the possibility of the San Dieguito district naming one of its junior high schools after Lt. Mitchell. Though not from the community, and having known him such a relatively short period of time, nontheless — if I may — that is an excellent idea.

No tribute given him will be fully adequate. His personal qualities, his drive, his zest for life can never be related, and the loss of Jim Mitchell, to his wife, his family, and his many friends, will never be compensated. America, as well as Encinitas, has lost one of its finest.

I, as do many of his friends, thank everyone for trying.
—1ST LT. BRIAN J. FAGAN, USMC,
1st Btn., 4th Marines,
S-1 (Btn. Adj.),
FPO, San Francisco 96601.

Editor's Note—Lt. Mitchell, of Encinitas, was killed in Viet Nam. His name was inscribed on a Palomar College plaque which will memorialize its students lost in action in Viet Nam. It has been proposed that a school in the San Dieguito union school district be named in his memory.

San Diego Evening Tribune, San Diego, California 1965

(Left to Right) Brian Fagan, Ed Howard, Jimmy Mitchell

> " No tribute given him will be fully adequate. His personal qualities, his drive, his zest for life can never be related, and the loss of Jim Mitchell to his wife, his family, and his many friends will never be compensated. "
>
> —1st Lt.Brian J. Fagan, USMC

69

Fallen Officer Is Praised

(Editor's note: The following letter was written to local newspapers from Captain Daniel A. Kelly, USMC. Capt. Kelly was the commanding officer of Lt. James M. Mitchell who was killed in August in Viet Nam. After his death there has been a movement to rename the present Solana Beach Junior High School (now Earl Warren Jr. High) in his honor. The following is the Captain's letter).

Dear Sir:

Information has reached me that the people of Encinitas are considering naming one of their Junior High Schools after the late Marine Lieutenant James M. Mitchell. Although not a member of your community, I feel that I speak for all in the Marine Corps who knew Jim Mitchell, in wholeheartedly endorsing your community's proposal.

I first met Jim in July of 1964 when I was assigned as Commanding Officer of "D" Company at Kaneohe Bay, Hawaii. Jim was platoon leader of our second platoon. Immediately I perceived that although fresh from officer training and with only two months in "D" Company, Lt. Mitchell had already won the respect of everyone who knew him. This accorded respect was the result of Jim's infectiously cheerful, enthusiastic approach to life in general and his job in particular, in addition to a respect for his fellow Marines that transcended all considerations of rank or position.

Besides Jim's work, he set a fine example for all in his personal life by his devotion to God and his family. Not only was Lt. Mitchell outstanding militarily, he was a most congenial friend, a superb athlete and all in all one of the finest men I have ever had the privilege to know.

During the better part of a year I watched Jim develop into the kind of a Marine and platoon leader that a Commander usually only dreams about. He was the kind of a man of whom any community could be justly proud. Lt. Mitchell demonstrated most clearly his excellent qualities when we went ashore at Chu Lai in Vietnam as he carefully guided his men through those difficult first days of combat. A couple of months after my subsequent transfer to Danang, I was shocked and extremely grieved by the news of Jim's death. But I was not at all surprised to learn that his death had been as generously devoted to his job and his men as had been his life.

For all of these reasons it seems particularly fitting that a school should bear the name of a young man whose life and death were a most eloquent assertion of what our nation's sometime maligned youth is and can be. But whether or not a community memorial is dedicated to the memory of Jim Mitchell, I will ever share with the people of Encinitas, a great pride in having been a part of his life and an even greater loss in his passing.—Captain Daniel A. Kelly, USMC.

> " "Not only was Lt. Mitchell outstanding militarily, he was a most congenial friend, a superb athlete and all in all one of the finest men I have ever had the privilege to know …"

"Besides Jim's work, he set a fine example for all in his personal life by his devotion to God and his family."

"… watched Jim develop into the kind of a Marine and platoon leader that a Commander usually only dreams about."

"But whether or not a community memorial is dedicated to the memory of Jim Mitchell, I will ever share with the people of Encinitas, a great pride in having been a part of his life and an even greater loss in his passing." "
— Captain Daniel A. Kelly, USMC

" … How are the Kelly's? Did Mrs. Kelly get her house sold? I told you Captain Kelly is working in Da Nang. I would like to see both Da Nang and Saigon before we leave here … "

Jimmy

Encinitas, California, October, 1965

Erin and I settled in an apartment sometime in October 1965. One afternoon I walked downstairs to my mailbox. When I took the mail from the box I looked briefly at the letters. To my complete shock, there was a letter to me from Jimmy. It was postmarked September 1, A.M. 1965. For several seconds my thoughts were excitement. For several brief seconds I knew someone had made a mistake—he was alive. I ran back to the apartment and opened the letter. By then reality had set in and I knew it was delayed mail. I had held on to some piece of hope. It was the last letter I ever received from him and I will never know if he received a letter from me before the sun went down in Chu Lai, Vietnam, on August 30, 1965.

Chu Lai, South Vietnam
30 August 11:00 A.M. (Postmarked September 1 A.M. 1965)
Dear Janny and Erin

I received your parents package yesterday and have already eaten — box of candy and plan to have chili for lunch. I also received the envelopes your sent. Thank you honey. It looks as though I may have to save them until I return to Oki as I will, after the 1st of Sept. be able to send letters without postage from here. Hope I won't have to use that privilege too long.

The mail service this past week has really been bad. I believe I have only received one letter from you in the last 6 days. It's too bad as I myself and just about everyone else looks forward to that mail each day. Hope they get the problem solved soon. I miss not hearing from my wife and daughter. Hope they are still writing to me.

I have sent these letters to your folks home as if the mail service is as bad going as it is coming, who knows when you will be reading this. How did you like the long letter, I just began writing and continued for a day or so. Was surprised when I tried to get the papers together. How do you like being back home? How did Erin take the move? She probably slept and ate through the whole event. Have you been eating regularly honey? You must in order to maintain your health.

6 P.M. We are getting ready for another night. I am sitting looking out of my house toward the mountains and all I can see are big black clouds. It looks as though the rain is really going to come down. We have a platoon size patrol tomorrow which is scheduled to last all day. We should be back about 4 in the afternoon. It has been quite a while since the platoon has been out on an operation, that is why I am getting fat. It will be good to get out for a day.

I am still hoping to get a letter from you tonight before the sun goes down. You know what honey, I love you and Erin also. Sure wish we were together, maybe soon. Please continue to write each day.

I love you Bird.
Jimmy

P.S. This should be the last time I have to use a stamp.
(referring to a postal franking privilege he was about to gain September 1.)

SEP
1
A.M.
1965

THE WHITE HOUSE
WASHINGTON

September 30, 1965

Dear Mrs. Mitchell:

It was with deep regret that I learned of the death of your
husband, First Lieutenant James M. Mitchell, Jr.,
United States Marine Corps, as the result of injuries received in action against hostile forces in Vietnam.

From the time your husband first entered the Marine Corps
to his latest assignment, he displayed outstanding professional skill and unselfish dedication to duty so essential to
a leader of men. His loyalty and many other exemplary
qualities won for him the admiration and respect of his
many friends and associates.

While I realize that words cannot lessen your grief, it is
my sincere hope that the memory of your husband's devoted
service will be a source of pride and comfort to you. This
Nation is deeply grateful for his contribution to its security.

Mrs. Johnson joins me in extending our heartfelt sympathy
to you in your tragic loss.

Sincerely,

Lyndon B. Johnson

Mrs. James M. Mitchell, Jr.
Encinitas, California

January 1st, 1966
Chu Lai, South Vietnam
Dear Jan & Erin,

Enclosed are two copies of the program for the Dedication Ceremony. It was conducted at 10:45 A.M., following Catholic Mass. Jim Peterson delivered the Eulogy, and I feel did a very good job in describing Jimmy to the <u>many</u> Marines present (By <u>many</u> I mean hundreds … !)

Be good, take care, say hi! to JoAnn & Kim, Caryll & Sara, and all the old gang. OK?

Bye for now. And … happy new year!
Brian Fagan

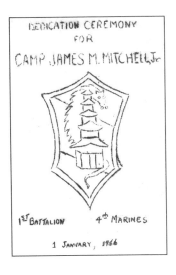

DEDICATION CEREMONY
FOR
CAMP JAMES M. MITCHELL Jr.

1ST BATTALION   4TH MARINES

1 JANUARY, 1966

THE POSTING OF COLORS

THE INVOCATION
Chaplain N. Hubble

THE EULOGY
Maj. R. M. Sweeney

THE DEDICATION OF THE CAMP
Lt. Col. R. J. Perrich

THE BENEDICTION
Chaplain W. B. Moody

THE SECURING OF COLORS

****

"Through God we shall do valiantly;
for He it is that shall tread down
our enemies." Psalms 60:12

****

Commanding Officer	Lt. Col. R.J.Perrich
Executive Officer	Maj. C. Romano
Sergeant Major	Sgt.Maj.D.C.Reeves

James M. MITCHELL, Jr. was born on 8 August 1940, in Seattle, Washington, grew up and attended school in the San Diego area. Upon his graduation in June 1963 from San Diego State University, and having completed training in the PLC program, he was commissioned a Second Lieutenant in the U. S. Marine Corps. Graduating from the Basic School, Quantico, Virginia, in March 1964, Lt. Mitchell reported to the 1st Battalion, 4th Marines, 1st Marine Brigade, FMF, for duty; on 28 May 1964, he was assigned as Platoon Commander, 2nd Platoon, Company "D". He served his Corps and his Country well, and was appointed a First Lieutenant on 5 December 1964. Lt. MITCHELL led his Platoon ashore at Chu Lai, Vietnam on 7 May. He participated extensively in combat operations against the Viet Cong, until on 31 August, 1965, while on a daylight combat patrol with his platoon, an enemy mine exploded directly in front of him, and Lt. MITCHELL was killed. May he rest in Peace.

January 1, 1966
Camp Dedication
Chu Lai, Vietnam

JIMMY MITCHELL VIET VICTIM

Father Would Be Pleased With His Daughter, Now 2

By PETER EIDEN

LEUCADIA—Erin Mitchell's world is one without a Vietnam. It is one of dolls and kiddie cars and nursery school.

It also is one without a father, except the man in the dress uniform she points to in a photo showing an arch of crossed sabers over a storybook bride and bridegroom.

Erin knows the handsome man in the dress uniform is her father only because her mother has told her so. Erin and her daddy never met.

FATHER KILLED

When Erin is older, she will learn about Vietnam, the place where Lt. Jimmy Mitchell stepped on a land mine on Aug. 31, 1965, and was killed. She was 6 weeks old then.

Blonde, pig-tailed Erin would rather have a daddy, but there are at least three perpetual memorials in his name: scholarship benefit basketball game at Palomar College, sportsmanship trophy at San Dieguito Union High School, and outstanding basketball player award at Palomar.

Her mother has a posthumous Purple Heart medal that Maj. Gen. Bruno Hochmuth presented, which is put away for Erin's future.

Those are bland substitutes, but there are many Erins in America today without fathers — few though from such a script of life that even fiction writers would find hard to conceive.

KIN OF ALCADE

Erin's mother is the former Jan Bertoncini, born in La Jolla Sept. 26, 1943, a great-great-granddaughter of Don Juan Maria Osuna, the first alcade of San Diego.

Erin's father, James M. Mitchell Jr., was born in Seattle Aug. 8, 1941. The stepson of a Marine colonel, he moved to this area as a child and lettered in football, track and basketball at San Dieguito High, then was a standout in basketball at Palomar Col-

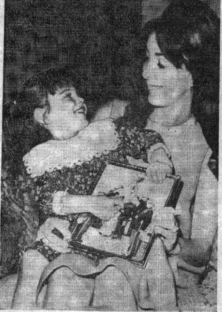

—Staff Photo by Pete Eiden
Mrs. Jimmy Mitchell shows daughter, Erin, 2, a photo of her daddy, who she will never know.

lege. He earned a bachelor's degree in business administration at San Diego State.

In high school, Mitchell met pretty brunette Jan Bertoncini.

"I went with Jim seven years before we were married," she said.

"We thought it was perfect. We had so many plans to do so many things together."

SWEETHEARTS WED

The high school sweethearts waited until Mitchell completed the rough platoon leaders course at Quantico, Va., and was commissioned before their marriage nearly four years ago — April 18, 1964 — in St. James Catholic Church at Del Mar.

Society columns acclaimed the wedding as something just short of Snow White's romance with Prince Charming: the marriage of all — but Jack Armstrong and the heiress to Rancho San Dieguito and whatever Osuna holdings there might be — although there were none left.

The young Mitchells had 11 months together at Kaneohe Bay, Hawaii, before he took a platoon to Chu Lai in Vietnam with the 1st Battalion, 4th Marine Regiment.

Blond-haired, blue-eyed Jimmy Mitchell — who had to look up to most of his juniors at 5 foot 4 and 145 pounds — was to go on patrol on Aug. 31, 1965.

JIMMY MITCHELL
. . . life was short

"I am sitting looking out toward the mountains and all I can see are big black clouds. We have a platoon size patrol tomorrow, scheduled to last all day. We should be back about 4 in the afternoon," Mitchell wrote his wife in the last letter she ever received.

It was dated Aug. 30. The letter carried a P.S., referring to a postal franking privilege he was about to gain Sept. 1. "This should be the last time I have to use a stamp."

It was. He was not back by 4.

"The Marine Corps life was it," Mrs. Mitchell recalls. "I never dreamed he would get killed. He was so devoted to the service."

She offers this advice to other women in similar circumstances.

"Keep busy, get out, do something. Mingle with people."

Mrs. Mitchell works part-time in a local doctor's office, takes golf lessons.

"To me, it was a tragedy," she said. "You just have faith. It was God's way. Jimmy believed in what he was doing."

— Afterward —

In 1991, Norm Kegerreis, who served in Jimmy's platoon, wrote a letter to Parade Magazine *in hopes of finding Erin and me.*

Hummelstown, Pennsylvania, 1991
To Whom It May Concern:

As a Vietnam veteran, I read with interest your coverage in *Parade*, and I can understand the anguish you must feel.

Many of us who served there saw fathers killed who never saw their child or children. We too have felt the pain and anguish and also guilt—often asking ourselves why this person who was a father was taken from us and his children when we who had no children survived.

The purpose of my letter is to ask you to search your membership files for a child who never knew his or her father. On August 31, 1965, my platoon leader, Lt. James Mitchell, was killed in action near Chu Lai, South Vietnam. I remember that in July '65 he was so proud of his first child being born and was showing everyone its picture. He never got to see that child. I do not know—or remember—if the child was a boy or girl. Lt. Mitchell was from Encinitas, California I have written to VFW and Legion posts in that area, but have had no luck in locating Lt. Mitchell's child.

If you could find someone in your files who might be his child, and he or she would like to contact me, I would have no problem with my address being forwarded to them. Thank you.

Sincerely,
Norm Kegerreis

The Response of Norm Kegerreis

Hummelstown, Pennsylvania, December 15, 1991
Dear Jan,

It was very nice of you to write. I never expected such a response. The thought of how you and Lt. Mitchell's child were had gnawed at me for years, and then when I received the information from "Vietnam in Touch,"

I thought I would at least make an attempt.

That day in August 1965 has always been vivid on my mind. I was some 60–80 feet away when the tragedy occurred. Lt. Mitchell was yelling for choppers to take out the wounded, and I thought he was okay. I was devastated when we learned differently. But even in that horrible moment, his concern was with others. That's how I'll always remember him—a caring, kind man. Although he wasn't tall in stature, he stood tall among us …

May you and Erin have a wonderful holiday season and give each other a hug from me.

Sincerely,
Norm Kegerreis

Hummelstown, Pennsylvania, … Later 1991

Dear Erin:

Thank you for responding to my letter. It was very good to hear from you.

Your father was my platoon leader and a very good one. Of all the people I served under in the Marine Corps, he was the best—a "Marine's marine." He was always concerned about the men he led, and we in turn would have followed him anywhere. Although he was a Lieutenant, he never made you feel he was better than you. Often he would stop by my position at night and chat. He was interested in how you were holding up, what your plans for the future were, etc.

Indirectly, I owe him my life or at least a life free of permanent maiming. Myself and a good friend of mine—Ed Beesley—both made Corporal at the same time. We both wanted to get off our squad because our squad leader was doing things we felt would get us killed. They didn't want two corporals in a squad, so one of us had to go. Ed felt that since he had been in the Marine Corps a week longer than me, he should be allowed to leave the squad. But your father said the only fair way was to draw straws. I won and moved to a mortar squad. On the day your father was killed in action, Ed was severely maimed—losing both legs from the knees down. I would have been in his position. It was the worst day of my life up until then and since. I still feel guilty about the incident. For whatever it's worth, at this late date, I prayed for you and your mom that night.

It seems as though those prayers were answered. Your mom endured, and you grew into a very good person. Your father would have been very proud of you. From what I can remember of him, you have his smile and his cheeks. Even though I don't really know you, I'm proud of you also.

Vietnam caused many of us to build a protective shell. Because we lost many close to us, we found it hard to get close to others upon our return for fear we'd probably lose them somehow …

—Norm Kegerreis

In May 1998, Wendy Haskett, who teaches a creative writing class and writes for the *North County Times* in Encinitas, Calif., wrote a very touching article about Jimmy. Two of the men who were on the patrol Aug. 31, 1965, read the article and contacted me through the newspaper: Sergeant Major Arthur "Sam" Fernandez, USMC (Ret.), and Ed Paulus. It was such a wonderful surprise knowing both men had settled in the North County area. Ed Paulus was kind enough to write his version of the incident and gave me the phone number for Ed Beesley in Edmond, Oklahoma.

Sam and his wife Fran met with me for breakfast one morning in Carlsbad, California. He was Jimmy's Platoon Sergeant. We talked for several hours, and he helped me to understand and visualize the scene that took place 36 years earlier.

Also in that year, a reunion was held in Las Vegas for officers of the 4th Marines who were in Hawaii in 1965 and left that same year for South Vietnam. There was an overwhelming feeling of warmth and nostalgia. I felt honored to be present for Jimmy. He was far from forgotten by the men who knew him.

February 12, 1999, Carlsbad, California

Jan:

I want to thank you for allowing me to write down a few of my thoughts about Lt. Mitchell. He was very special and was loved by all of the men in his command. I also want to tell you how much I appreciate you "thanking me" for serving in Vietnam. You are only the second person in my life to do so and coming from you it means the world to me.

The platoon was called to attention, and he walked into our lives. At first we thought just another "boot Lieutenant" to put up with, but we were soon to find out otherwise. This Lieutenant not only demanded respect and loyalty from us but gave it back to us in trump! He never demanded more from us than he was willing to give himself. In all the months of training and eventual combat we saw, there was never a day that I didn't thank God to have him leading us.

When we landed in Vietnam, the attitude was that we would "kick butt" and go home heroes. That quickly disappeared with the first casualties we experienced. Lt. Mitchell always had a way of getting us through the trauma and keeping us focused on the mission at hand. As mundane as that may sound to some, I am convinced it made the difference in our ability to cope from day to day.

The tedium of countless patrols and operations would be punctuated by occasional firefights and worse, encounters with booby-traps designed to maim or kill its victims as well as leaving the more fortunate of us demoralized.

On a hot August day in 1965 we encountered our darkest day. While on patrol in an area dreaded for its abundance of such traps, the unthinkable occurred. My squad was guarding the right flank when the word came down for Lt. Mitchell to come up to the point. The explosion knocked me to my knees. When my ears stopped ringing all I could hear were screams of agony. By the time I reached the point, Lt. Mitchell was gone, and we were busy applying first aid to the other casualties. I was told after that Lt. Mitchell had gotten to his feet and said something to the effect that "these men need help" and then collapsed. Although I don't know this for sure, it would have been true to his character. He always thought of his men first. We walked out of the jungle that day with tears in our eyes and a feeling of tremendous loss.

A few weeks later we were present for the dedication of a base camp in Lt. Mitchell's name. We stood at rigid attention, with tears in our eyes, as his heroics were read.

Whenever I hear mention of his size I just laugh for he was the "biggest" man I ever knew, and I still miss him.

Respectfully,
Ed Paulus
Former Squad Leader
Delta Co., 1st Battalion, 4th Marines

In October 2000, I flew to Oklahoma City to meet with Ed Beesley and his wife Connie. Norm Kegerreis drove from his home in Enola, Pennsylvania to join us. Our meeting had finally taken place. It was an emotional time for the four of us. We spent three days together getting to know one another and sharing many hours discussing the events of August 31, 1965. I had wanted to hear the story of Jimmy's death from someone who had been present at the time of the explosion. Ed was able to relate the experience to me. He was firm in his statement that Jimmy's death was caused by shrapnel from the same mine that took both his own legs from above the knees. In all, it took two lives and both legs from three men.

Seeing Ed in a wheelchair as a double amputee was disturbing at first. As the hours passed, I could see a man who had survived the loss of both legs and survived very well. As I watched Ed wrestle with his grandchildren on the living room floor, and listened to his sermon as Pastor to Edmond Grace Fellowship Church in Edmond, Oklahoma I felt a sense of relief.

Norm Kegerreis left Vietnam and fought his own mental battle from the war. He too, is a survivor. He retired after 25 years as a police officer.

Jan, Norm Kegerreis, Connie and Ed Beesley

A life not forgotten

July 98

PHOTO COURTESY OF JAN MITCHELL MEYER

Encinitas woman still trying to understand husband's death

"**I**'ve been looking for you for years," the man told Jan Mitchell Meyer over the telephone. His name, he said, was Norm Kegerreis. He'd been a corporal in her husband's platoon in Vietnam. "I just wanted to tell you what an outstanding Marine Lt. Mitchell was. I've never forgotten him."

"As I thanked him," Jan says, "I was thinking how often I'd heard someone use the words — 'I've never forgotten him' — when they were talking about Jim."

"He was excited about the baby," Kegerreis said. "A girl, right?"

"I told him, yes, that Erin was 29 now. She'd been only six weeks when Jim was killed at Chu Lai, when a land mine exploded. He never saw her, although I had managed to get a photograph to him through the Red Cross."

Kegerreis, she realized, was still talking: "He was telling me that Jim hadn't been killed instantly, as I'd always believed. I knew he'd been hit in the heart by mine fragments. This man, who'd been a stranger minutes before, was telling me that he'd been there, on that patrol, that Jim had struggled to his feet, and begun shouting orders to his men, trying to sort out the chaos, before he dropped."

Jan with her three grandchildren, left to right: Ally, Jan, Chase and Kye.

May 24, 1998
Quotes From The North County Times

A Life Not Forgotten by Wendy Haskett

"Jimmy was special—it's hard to describe what he had if you didn't know him," his friend, Mike Shores, who played on the same basketball team, says.

"At one of our basketball games, someone on the opposing team called out something derogatory about Jimmy's height—he was 5 feet 5 inches, which is really unusual in basketball. Mitchell bounced the ball between the guy's legs, zipped around him, started dribbling it. No one could catch him —you could never get a ball away from him—so the crowd was roaring with laughter. But after the game, he was friendly to the guy who insulted him. That was Jimmy. You couldn't play with the guy and not be up."

North County newspapers at that time contained letters from people who wanted to rename Earl Warren Junior High the James Mitchell Junior High.

"It didn't happen," Mike Shores says. "But San Dieguito High named the new auditorium after him."

6 November 1998

Dear Jan,

The 4th Marines Reunion in Las Vegas brought back so many memories of Kaneohe Bay and our early days in Vietnam. Our experiences during that very challenging period most certainly shaped how we viewed our most personal relationships with fellow Marines and with our families. We dedicated ourselves to being the best Marines and the best husband and father and so often found those roles in competition with each other. I know there were times when you and Sandra wondered what you had signed up for.

When Jim joined 1st Battalion, I had moved up to the Regimental staff but continued to associate myself with Jim and his peers as though I was still a battalion officer. Jim really did stand out – he had an engaging personality, well founded self-confidence and an athletic ability that few could match. As I viewed him from a distance I was certain his Marines admired him greatly and would follow him anywhere.

Vietnam was not a bad experience for all who served there – we quickly came to know what we were made of and we were witness to all of the best of human qualities. We were unaffected by the protesters on the home front and simply sought to execute our mission successfully and bring our Marines home safely. You know that Jim was doing everything possible to bring his Marines home safely and most certainly was leading from the front when he was killed.

There are events in our lives that stand out so clearly in our memory and I must tell you that I will never forget where I was when the word of Jim's death reached us. To this day when I hear mention of Vietnam and those who died there I think of Jim. I thought of you as though you might be Sandra and always wondered how you had survived. Seeing you at the reunion answered that – I was so pleased to see your name on the roster of attendees and wish it had not taken us so long to reconnect. If your travels bring you to Tucson you know you have friends to visit.

Erin surely knows that her father was an exceptional man.

Sincerely,

Bob Johnston

Robert B. Johnston
Lieutenant General, USMC (Ret)

October 30, 2000
Ed Beesley's Memories

(Approximately 6 miles northwest of Chu Lai Airfield, RVN)

The day started out as did many other days. My squad had been on patrol during the night. The men (I say men—some of them were 17 and 18 years old) were exhausted and needed to rest but that would not happen today. By 7:00 A.M. Lt. Mitchell had already received his orders from the company CO and had called all the squad leaders together. Today we would go on a platoon sized patrol.

Our squad was informed that we would take point today. My squad leader (Sergeant Belcher) yelled "Beesley you're on point." Being raised on a farm, I grew up with a natural sense of direction, therefore, I was called on quite often to walk point. Today for the first time since becoming a Marine, I would refuse to follow an order from a superior. After a heated argument with my squad leader, I was assured by my platoon Sergeant that as an E4 and having only a couple of months before I was scheduled to go home, I would not be called on to walk point again. I agreed to take the point this one last time.

We padded up and headed north and a little west of our position at the north end of the Chu Lai air strip. We had gone about six miles when we came to a hedge row. As I stepped through the hedge I spotted a land mine laying on the ground about 25 or 30 meters in front of me. The hole had been dug but the mine had not been planted.

I held up the column, we were in a mine field. I passed the word back to Lt. Mitchell. He came to check the situation. He and Corporal Duffey came through the hedge to my left and were standing about 15 feet from the mine. As I waited for the Lieutenant to decide what we should do, a squad leader from another squad walked past me on the narrow trail. As he passed by he bumped my shoulder slightly, I took a step backward to regain my balance. As I stepped back I looked down at the ground. I had stepped on another mine. I saw it come out of the ground between my feet. It was a Bouncing Betty type mine. The explosion threw me several feet into the air and I fell on my back. There was blood and pieces of flesh everywhere. I grabbed my head with both hands, it was still there. As I looked down at my feet all I saw was jagged shin bones with no flesh on them.

As a young corpsman worked on me I could not see what was happening but I could hear Lt. Mitchell yelling out orders to set up a perimeter and to call for Medevac. The older corpsman was with Lt. Mitchell and Corporal Duffy. The next thing I heard was the older corpsman screaming, "He's dying." Someone yelled, "Shut him up." He continued to scream. The next voice yelled, "Hit him, knock him out." The screaming stopped.

The young corpsman and others from the platoon frantically worked on the wounded. I could hear Ed Paulus yelling, "where are those choppers?" Sergeant Bolt and Gene Burns lay close by. Both had severe wounds to the legs. Foster had been hit but seemed to be okay.

My legs felt like they were on fire, I was so tired. I could hear the choppers …

Ed Beesley (Age 19) in Recovery
Oakland Naval Hospital, Oakland, California

Ed Beesley, October, 2000
Oklahoma City, Oklahoma

October, 2000
Norm Kegerreis' Memories

Lieutenant Jimmy Mitchell was the platoon leader for the second platoon. Back then we called him Mr. Mitchell. A short compact man with an infectious smile. He also had this look when something worried or concerned him. But he made decisions without hesitation. We looked up to him and felt safe under his leadership. He did not act like he was better than those who served under him. He was concerned about each of us. On one occasion, I went to him with a problem and he took care of it. In Hawaii, I had started a correspondence course in Conservation. When we headed to Vietnam, I packed my books up and stored them. Some four months later, I received a notice demanding payment, and it disturbed me. Mr. Mitchell had a friend in legal, and he took care of it. I never again heard anything from the school. On another occasion, he found me sleeping on watch and told me to report to him in the morning. When I did, he told me he never knew what I did but he would have to discipline me. Everyone in my fireteam was tired that night because we had just gotten back from a two-day patrol. I told my team I would take the first watch but at some point I decided I would stay up all night and let everyone sleep. But I ended up falling asleep. Mr. Mitchell sent me to the ammo dumps for eight hours—loading and unloading crates of ammo. I respected his decision and never held any animosity toward him.

When his daughter was born in July, he shared his joy with everyone—not just his fellow officers. How proud he was to be a Daddy!

And then, on the morning of 31 August 1965, 2nd Platoon went on a patrol near Chu Lai. My friend, Ed Beesley, and I were some 60 to 80 feet apart. Suddenly, there was a loud explosion and everything came to a standstill. The explosion went some 80 feet into the air. Someone yelled we were in a mine field. There was a lot of screaming and confusion. I heard Lieutenant Mitchell yelling for choppers. There was no indication that he himself was in trouble. The explosion killed Corporal Duffy outright, mortally wounded Lieutenant Mitchell and blew the legs off my friend, Corporal Beesley, among others. Eventually all were evacuated. Later, we learned that Lieutenant Mitchell died.

That night was the darkest night of my life. I cried. I thought about the child who would grow up without a father, the young wife and what this would do to her. And Ed Beesley, who loved to run but now could never do so again. My tour of duty in Vietnam ended that day because for my last four months I can't remember the people or the places. I volunteered for extra patrols. I just wanted to get it over with.

When I passed through California on my way home, I wanted to stop and see the widow and the child. I used the excuse I didn't know where they were living but in reality I was afraid. As the years turned into decades I thought of both often. There was always this unfulfilled need to meet them—to know that they were safe. I decided it was time.

October 17, I finally met the child. Erin, you are special—not just to me but to others. You are delightful as is your family. Your Dad would be very proud. Somehow I know that he has looked over you all these years. I hope you can understand why after all these years myself and Ed wanted to meet you. We all share a common bond and that bond was broken on August 31, 1965, but most of all we did it for your Dad.

(Left to Right) Ally Lauren, Erin, Kye Mitchell, Norm Kegerreis, Chase Meyer (October 17, 2000)

Ed Beesley with Erin

In May 2001, Ed and Connie made a special trip to Durham, North Carolina to meet Erin and her family. When Ed returned to his home in Edmond, he called to tell me about their visit. He said, "It was the highlight of my life." Thirty-six years gone by and he had finally been able to sit with Erin and tell her the story of August 31, 1965. As he had told me, he told Erin that he had gone over and over that day hundreds of times in his mind. He said he had absolutely done everything "by the book." I asked Erin to drop me a line telling me how she felt about their visit:

"I had the opportunity to meet with Ed Beesley and his wife Connie this past week. I was nervous at first not knowing what to expect but after spending a great deal of time with them I walk away with a better understanding of the Vietnam War, of the conditions that these men endured, the homecoming they received after sacrificing their life for our freedom, the politics involved, and most importantly, of the relationship that these men had with my father and his integrity and character that was true until the end of his short life. I am so impressed and so grateful that these men have taken the time to share some of the details of this terrible war that only they know. I told Ed that it is hard for me to understand it all because I did not live it. I am so blessed to have a wonderful husband, terrific children, and the support of family and friends. It is my Dad that I grieve for. He never had the opportunity to experience a first smile, a first tooth, a first LOST tooth, Little League, etc. etc. … all the joys that come with taking your child into adulthood. Ed is amazing."

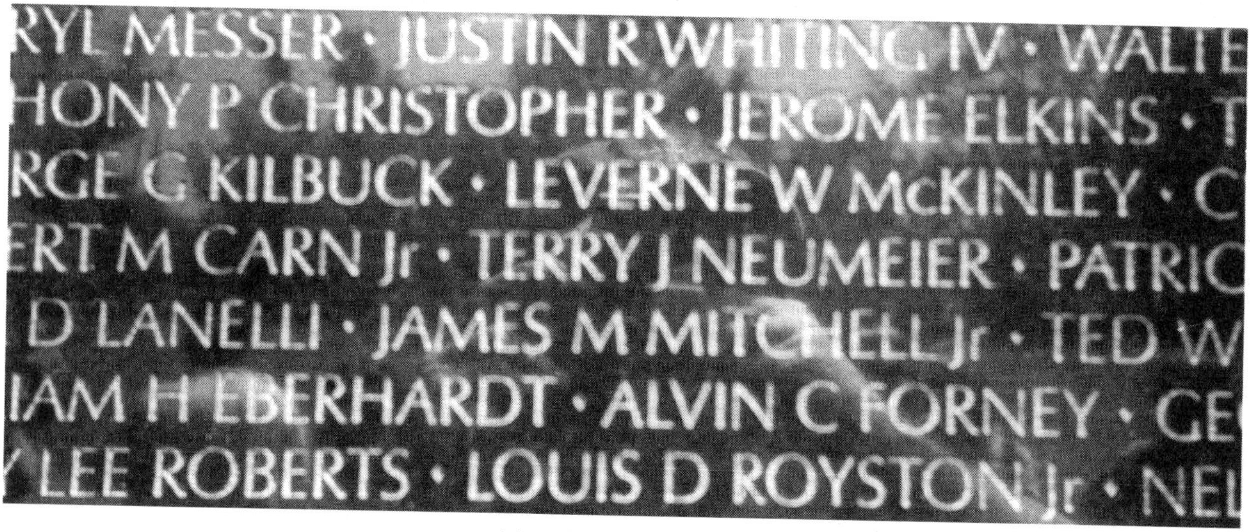

"The Wall," Washington, D.C.

January 2002

Through the years I watched Erin grow from the tiny baby in the pink terry cloth jump suit, to a beautiful young lady both inside and out. It always astounds me to watch her movements. She has her father's features and his zest for life. Her laugh, her walk and mannerisms are just like him. She graduated from Arizona State University in Tempe, Arizona in 1987 and was employed for a period of time with America West Airlines as a Flight Service Manager on the Boeing 747. During that time, she had the privilege of flying to Belgium to assist the men who were flying home from the Desert Storm war.

In 1993, she married Scott Rhode. They have three children and live in Longview, Texas. Now I watch my only granddaughter, Ally, growing into the little girl that resembles Erin. When I see my grandchildren at play I sometimes find my mind wandering back to the days of high school, falling in love with

Erin with Jan, 1967

Erin with Ally, 1999

their grandfather, and the happy days we had on the beautiful Island of Oahu.

On November 10, 2001, the 226th anniversary of the United States Marine Corps was celebrated. Ed Beesley was the guest of honor for the event that was held in Tulsa, Oklahoma. He invited Erin and I to attend. Ed spoke in front of 500 Marines and their guests. I turned to Erin and whispered, "Who would have ever thought we'd be here tonight 36 years later."

For everything, thank you, Jimmy Mitchell.

226th Anniversary

Jan and Erin with Ed Beesley
at the Marine Corps Birthday Ball, 2001

Brooklyn Bridge, New York City, 1999
Front Lt. To Rt.: Kye, Ally, Chase. Back Row: Scott and Erin Rhode

6 August 1965

… How are my girls? Smiling all the time and having lots of fun I hope.

Love, Dad

Erin and Jan

A Special Thank You

I met Kay Vickers in 1997 while I was doing some work for hospice. Kay had written her own life story and thus directed me to StoryArts, who had helped her write and publish her book. She knew their assistance would be just what I needed to help me also write and publish Jim's story.

As I began writing his story, Kay continuously rallied me on whenever I was discouraged. Her support, plus the guidance and expertise of Lois Sunrich and Doris Doi at StoryArts, as well as Suzanna Neal's generous support led to the book's completion. I am so grateful to you all.

PHOTO CREDITS:

Cover photo by Buster Toland, Gunnery Sergeant USMCR, (Ret.), 1965

Pages 16–17: From 1959 San Dieguito High School Hoofprint Yearbook

Page 19: Jimmy Mitchell, age 19, Encinitas, CA,
      Photo Courtesy of Mr. and Mrs. Butch Stillman

Page 27: 430 North Kalaheo Kailua, Hawaii,
      Photo Courtesy of Nancy Rodhouse Bossidy, 1973

Page 86: Ed Beesley, age 19, Photo Courtesy of Connie Beesley, 2001

Page 89: Ed Beesley with Erin, Photo Courtesy of Connie Beesley, 2001

Page 90: "The Wall," Washington, D.C., Photo Courtesy of Norm Kegerreis, 2000

Page 92: Marine Ball, Photo Courtesy of © Cornellius Photocraft, Tulsa, Oklahoma

Page 93: Brooklyn Bridge, New York City, 1999, Photo Courtesy of Angelika Hudson

Page 95: Erin and Jan, Photo by Shannen L. Morgan, Durham, North Carolina © 2001

*1st edition published
by StoryArts, Inc.
Leucadia, CA*

*Book Design by
Doris Doi,
San Diego, CA*

StoryArts, Inc.

In January of 1990, a group of 31 women came together to write in their diaries. Twelve years later, Storymakers, which we named ourselves, still meets monthly to write, share and celebrate life. It is out of our commitment to write honestly, listen deeply and support each other's vision of our lives, that StoryArts was born.

Today, StoryArts offers people in every walk of life the opportunity to shape hard earned daily life events into stories that recognize and maintain meaning in life. We help families, elders, teens … anyone with a story to share, produce high quality books and videos that they can give to their families and friends. We are a small and intimate, nonprofit consortium of custom publishers and video artists dedicated to honoring, archiving and celebrating life's stories.